THE BEST ADVICE EVER

FOR BECOMING A

SUCCESS AT WORK

THE BEST ADVICE EVER

FOR BECOMING A

SUCCESS AT WORK

ROBERT McCORD

**Andrews McMeel
Publishing**

Kansas City

01 02 03 04 05 QUF 10 9 8 7 6 5 4 3 2 1

Library of Congress Cataloging-in-Publication Data

McCord, Robert R.
    The best advice ever for becoming a success at work /
[compiled by] Robert McCord.
        p. cm.
    Includes bibliographical references.
    ISBN 0-7407-1409-0
        1. Success—Psychological references. 2. Success in
business. I. Title.

BF637.S8 M35 2001
650.14—dc21   2001046078

For Belinda,
the successful owner of
San Francisco Top Models
and Talent, with love

CONTENTS

Acknowledgments
• ix •

Introduction
• xi •

Strategy and
Business Planning
• 1 •

Management
• 10 •

Leadership
• 26 •

Human Resources
• 36 •

Careers
• 43 •

The Workplace
• 53 •

Finance and Accounting
• 65 •

The Customer
• 78 •

Sales and Marketing
• 85 •

Advertising and
Public Relations
• 96 •

Products and Branding
• 108 •

Pricing
• 113 •

Competition
• 116 •

Operations, Productivity,
and Distribution
• 121 •

Research and
Development
• 127 •

Meetings and Negotiations
• 132 •

Business Trends
• 136 •

Government and Business
• 141 •

The Global Economy
• 146 •

Entrepreneurship
• 155 •

Technology and the Web
• 162 •

The Law, Ethics, and
Social Responsibility
• 171 •

ACKNOWLEDGMENTS

I would like to thank Patrick Dobson, my editor, and the staff at Andrews McMeel Publishing for all of their support for this book.

Thanks to David McCormick, my agent and friend at IMG. And a note of appreciation to the faculty and my colleagues at the MBA program at Columbia University, especially the West Side Study Group, which gave me insight into business and its many interesting facets. Also, thanks to Ron Janoff, former director of the Management Institute at New York University; my various colleagues at my sundry employers Baker & Taylor, Scholastic, International Thomson, Prentice-Hall, Grolier, populardemand, inc.; and my consulting and publishing clients who have provided support and an appreciation for the world of business.

Also, affectionate appreciation to Belinda Irons, the owner of San Francisco Top Models and Talent, who has provided me with love and support for this and many other endeavors.

INTRODUCTION

The world of business and work has evolved from relatively simple agrarian self-sufficiency to a complex world of high technology and global organizations.

Whereas in the old days it took a strong back, a keen sense of judgment, and a robust work ethic to put bread on the table, now it often takes a strong intellect, an advanced degree, and managerial, political, and a whole range of other skills. Modern business and the workplace have evolved into a post-industrial knowledge and service industry where innovation and brainpower are the keys to success.

Parallel to the rise in sophistication and complexity of business is the development of a variety of sources of information and advice on how to more effectively develop and manage enterprises. Among these sources are business school professors, stock analysts, investment gurus, books, magazines, seminars, newsletters, the Web, and other media. Business icons such as Peter Drucker, Jack Welch, Warren Buffet, Theodore Levitt, Faith Popcorn, Peter Lynch, Mark McCormack, and others have become household names for those with any interest in business. Books like *The Organization Man, What They Don't Teach You at Harvard Business*

School, The Peter Principle, The One Minute Manager, Positioning, What Color Is Your Parachute? and *The New New Thing* have become classics that provide insight into how organizations operate and how a manager can navigate that environment.

Many business commentators paint a candid but grim picture of what it is like to be in the trenches. Michael Maccoby, author of *The Gamesman,* relates: "Why are corporate managers fearful? Some are frightened that they will fail to perform well; they will lose a sale, miss a deadline, come up with the wrong answer. Someone above them will decide they don't measure up and 'zap' them. . . . Even if they are not afraid of being fired or sent to Siberia, they worry that by not moving ahead, they will fall behind and be forgotten. The company will discover that they are not needed."

Other observers, such as Steven M. Pollan and Mark Levine in their book, *Die Broke,* are similarly skeptical about the atmosphere of the modern workplace: "Concerned with personal growth, you looked for work that was 'challenging' and that allowed for 'self-expression.' This self-fulfillment ethic makes a great deal of sense, if it's built upon a foundation of job security. But today, with insecurity the rule, the continued pursuit of self-fulfillment leads to incredible frustration." Michael Ovitz, a noted Hollywood agent who was briefly an executive at Disney, takes this approach to business competition: "The whole forward momentum thing is such a key part of my nature. You just keep pushing ahead, no matter what. It's like *Private Ryan*—you can't stop and say 'This guy's dead,' or else you're going to be dead." Other commentators, such as Bob Nelson in *1,001*

Ways to Take the Initiative at Work and Beverly Rokes in *Quick Skills: Embracing Diversity,* offer positive helpful managerial hints to cope with obstacles in the business environment.

Perhaps as a backlash to some of the limitations of conventional corporate life, entrepreneurship has blossomed, especially as represented by the development of home businesses and the Internet. It remains to be seen whether the Web can be a profitable business for many, but it is clear that the Internet has added depth and breadth to the one-world global economy concept. At the same time all is not high tech and affluence. Millions of people are living below the poverty line and suffer from disease, malnutrition, and other deprivations caused by natural and man-made disasters. C. Michael Armstrong, CEO of Hughes Electronics, noted in 1997: "Fewer than half the population of the world, about three billion people, have never placed a phone call; at the most 50 percent enjoy daily access to electrical power, and fewer than 11 percent of the world's people have owned a car." This raises the question of social responsibility that business, government, and other institutions have toward improving human conditions. As you would expect, some businesses are better at it than others.

Contained in this book is a fair share of rueful commentary about the pitfalls of business and the workplace. But, for the most part, the emphasis is on problem solving and overcoming obstacles. The book is organized into a series of sections reflective of the structure and dynamic of business. I have cited well-known experts on management such as Philip Kotler, Theodore Levitt, Theodore Drucker, and others, as well as lesser known sources who provide insight into the world of commerce. At the same time I have drawn on nonbusiness sources such as the Bible, Plato, de Tocqueville, Mark Twain, Woody Allen, and others who, perhaps, provide more insight into the human condition and why people behave the way they do in business situations.

I hope you will find some sustenance in these pages to assist you in appreciating the sometimes confusing, but never dull, world of business.

—Robert R. McCord, New York City, 2001

STRATEGY AND BUSINESS PLANNING

These are the four steps that companies can follow to find a corporate soul and win the consumer's heart in the '90s:

Acknowledgment: Our industry hasn't always done everything in its power to make the world a better place.

Disclosure: This is who we were. And this is the company we're trying, with your help, to become.

Accountability: Here is how we define our arena of responsibility, and who can be held accountable.

Presentation: Here is what we pledge to you, the consumer: you'll find our corporate soul in all our products.

—Faith Popcorn,
The Popcorn Report *(1991)*

In the arena of human life the honors and rewards fall to those who show their good qualities in action.

—*Aristotle, in* The Forbes Book of Business Quotations, *edited by Ted Goodman (1997)*

Most business plans have a fairly standard structure. We can think of the structure as a table of contents with various chapter headings. Most plans tend to have more or less the same chapters, usually called sections. Each section addresses a major business issue or function: marketing, finance, production, etc. It's useful to think of each section as a component of the business, and understand that a plan, just like a business, must have all of its components in working order to be effective. For example, virtually all plans have sections showing financial projections, on marketing and management. What's in the sections differs according to the business.

—*William Lasher, Ph.D., CPA,* The Perfect Business Plan Made Simple *(1994)*

No institution which does not continually test its ideals, techniques, and measure of accomplishment can claim real vitality.

—*John Milton, in* The Forbes Book of Business Quotations, *edited by Ted Goodman (1997)*

All men dream . . . but not equally. They who dream by night in the dusty recesses of their minds wake in the day to find that it is vanity; but the dreamers of the day are dangerous men, for they act their dream with open eyes, to make it possible.

—*T. E. Lawrence (1888–1935)*

[Steve] Jobs clearly said the right words. He defined Apple's culture as "other-directed" [changing the world], but the company was just as clearly focused inward. The company's strategy and actions reflected its real values: to keep others out, to build a bastion of Apple-based users. Oddly, about the same time, IBM was making a similar blunder regarding the mainframe computer. IBM's declared values were also impressive, calling for "the best customer service in the world," but the company ignored the customers' clear desire for a distributed environment supported by personal computers. Apple and IBM started to believe that they could control a major portion of the world of computing. They both shifted their focus from the customer to themselves, trying to partition that world to serve their own needs. Therein lies the mistake of perspective: they forgot to take their own values seriously when they developed these business strategies.

—David S. Pottruck and Terry Pearce,
Clicks and Mortar: Passion Driven Growth
in an Internet Driven World *(2000)*

Vision is the art of seeing things invisible.

—Jonathan Swift (1667–1745)

Rolex is not in the watch business. We are in the luxury business.

—Andre Heineger, chairman of Rolex, in
What They Don't Teach You at Harvard
Business School *by Mark McCormack (1984)*

It is no wonder that many CEOs complain that their marketing isn't working. They see their company spending more on marketing and accomplishing less. One reason is that they are spending more on the same old type of marketing that they have in the past. Neanderthal marketing consists of the following practices:

- Equating marketing and selling.
- Emphasizing customer acquisition rather than customer care.
- Trying to make a profit on each transaction rather than trying to profit by managing customer lifetime value.
- Pricing based on marking up cost rather than target pricing.
- Planning each communication tool separately rather than integrating marketing communication tools.
- Selling product rather than trying to understand and meet the customer's real needs.

—*Philip Kotler,* Kotler on Marketing *(1999)*

The first step in deciding how to position your product is to select your target market segment. An example is McDonald's decision to go after young adults who are heavy users of fast-food restaurants. A target market segment comes from first recognizing that different groups, or segments, of the market have different needs and wants. Kids versus adults. And heavy users of fast food versus light users. Each of these distinctions cuts the population into groups. Add the two distinctions together and you have a two-dimensional segmentation of your market.

—*Alexander Hiam,* Marketing for Dummies *(1997)*

To me golf is like the restaurant business. You make money at the bottom, like at McDonald's, and you make money at the top, like at Lutece. But you starve in the middle.

—Gerald Barton, chairman of the Landmark Land Company (1991)

To get things done it's important to set goals, but what is the difference between a good goal and one that misses the mark? The best goals are:

- Few in number, specific in focus
- Not too hard, not too easy
- Mutually agreed upon, with others who will work toward the goal
- Visualized and written down

And when it comes to deciding exactly what goals to focus on, ask yourself the questions:

- What actions give you the greatest impact?
- What one thing will you do differently?
- How will you keep your commitment to doing that one thing?

—Bob Nelson, 1,001 Ways to Take the Initiative at Work *(1999)*

Trends will come and trends will go, but meeting the needs of your consumer, taking care of your employees and being responsible to the communities in which we live and work are basic values that will never go out of style. They will also lead to long-term gains for any corporation's stockholders. These principles, embodied in the one-hundred-year-old Johnson & Johnson credo, will still be in style in one hundred years.

—Brian D. Perkins, director of product management, McNeil Consumer Products Co., in The Popcorn Report *by Faith Popcorn (1991)*

If your only tool is a hammer, everything looks like a nail.

>—*Nathan C. Myhrvold, chief of R&D,*
>*Microsoft, in* Fortune *(1993)*

Using feminine principles in business is wonderful—leading a company with gut feelings, instinct, intuition, passion. Very strong female ethics revolve around the concept of caring and sharing, and I still believe that women can change the marketplace.

>—*Anita Roddick, managing director of*
>*the Body Shop PLC, in* The Popcorn Report
>*by Faith Popcorn (1991)*

His old thinking had been clouded by his worries and fears. He used to think about not having enough cheese, or not having it last as long as he wanted. He used to think more about what could go wrong than what could go right. . . .

Now he realized it was natural for change to continually occur, whether you expect it or not. Change could surprise you only if you didn't expect it and weren't looking for it.

When he realized he had changed his beliefs, he paused to write on the wall: Old Beliefs Do Not Lead You To New Cheese.

>—*Spencer Johnson, M.D.,* Who Moved My Cheese? *(1998)*

At IBM Gerstner flashed a large photograph of Microsoft Corp. chairman Bill Gates on a screen. "This man wakes up hating you," he snapped at his managers. "The message: you've got to hate him back."

>—*Stanley Bing,* What Would Machiavelli Do? *(2000)*

Change has become a way of life for many companies. But is change the way to keep pace with change? The exact opposite appears to be true. The landscape is littered with the debris of projects that companies rushed into in attempting to keep pace. . . . Meanwhile the programs of those who kept at what they did best and held their ground have been immensely successful. Maytag selling its reliable appliances. Walt Disney selling the world of fantasy and fun. Avon calling.

—Al Ries and Jack Trout, Positioning *(2001)*

An organization which just perpetuates today's level of vision, excellence, and accomplishment has lost the capacity to adapt. And since the one and only thing certain in human affairs is change, it will not be capable of survival in a changed tomorrow.

—Peter Drucker, The Effective Executive *(1999)*

I dream for a living.

—Steven Spielberg, film director, in Fortune *(1996)*

The Wal-Mart formula is deceptively simple: Sell good quality, name-brand, modestly priced merchandise in a clean, no-frills setting that offers one-stop family shopping. Rather than entice shoppers with an ever-changing array of discounts and sales, Wal-Mart operated from an "everyday low price" philosophy. It sends out few advertising circulars, and the ones it does are positioned as shopping reminders— they contain no off-price specials. Not only does this pricing stability cut advertising costs and contribute to the kind of lean overhead that lends itself to price-competitive retailing, it also creates an image of dependability and, if you will, fair play in the minds of customers. At Wal-Mart, you don't have the nagging doubt that what you're buying might have cost you less last week, or might go on sale next Sunday.

> —*Ron Zemke with Dick Schaaf,*
> The Service Edge: 101 Companies That
> Profit from Customer Care *(1989)*

Innovating companies today are using their balanced scorecards to:
1. gain consensus and clarity about their strategic objectives,
2. communicate strategic objectives to business units, departments, teams, and individuals,
3. align strategic planning, resource allocation, and budgeting processes, and
4. obtain feedback and learn about the effectiveness of their strategic plan and its implementation.

> —*Robert S. Kaplan and David P. Norton,*
> The Balanced Scorecard: Translating
> Strategy into Action *(1996)*

The bourgeoisie, by the rapid improvement of all instruments of production, by the immensely facilitated means of communication, draws all, even the most barbarian, nations into civilisation. The cheap prices of its commodities are the heavy artillery with which it batters down all Chinese walls; with which it forces the barbarians' intensely obstinate hatred of foreigners to capitulate. It compels all nations, on pain of extinction, to adopt the bourgeois mode of production; it compels them to introduce what it calls civilisation into their midst, i.e., to become bourgeois themselves. In one world, it creates a world after its own image. . . .

—*Karl Marx and Friedrich Engels,*
The Communist Manifesto *(1848)*

They started in the shoe business. You fit shoes on people. You go get shoes for them. You put them on their feet. All this makes for a culture that personally serves people. As Nordstrom evolved into a specialty department store it maintained some of that personal attention. Nordstrom people run for the customer. Part of it comes from that. Part of it comes from the family commitment to service. Nordstrom hasn't had a revolving door with executives with ten different philosophies. It has a consistent philosophy. And that gets communicated when hiring people.

—*Larry Senn of Senn-Delaney, a retail consulting firm, speculating on the genesis of Nordstrom's high service standards (1986)*

MANAGEMENT

I prefer to deal with strong egos, as I'm sure most business people do. These are usually the executives who are willing to take reasonable risks, don't second-guess, and are the quickest to get things done. Weaker egos are harder to read, which makes it more difficult to determine your own course of action. They also operate with lower expectations of themselves. . . . which means that dealing with them will take more time and will accomplish less. . . . Instead of always challenging or confronting the other person's ego, it is much easier and far more effective to acknowledge and understand its impact on your business and use this information to your advantage.

—*Mark McCormack,* What They
Don't Teach You at Harvard
Business School *(1984)*

Mr. Morgan buys his partners; I grow my own.

—Andrew Carnegie, founder of Carnegie Steel,
in Life of Andrew Carnegie *by Burston J. Hendrick (1932)*

Our analysis found strong evidence suggesting that boards which adopt certain key attributes are able to govern more effectively and produce superior company financial performance. These attributes include the following:

- Information about a broad set of indicators of organizational effectiveness and about how these indicators compare with the performance of leading firms in the company's sector.
- Knowledge of the key technological and market changes affecting the firm's future power to counter-balance top management, which can be maintained by ensuring that outsiders hold a clear majority of board positions, control the marketing agenda, and conduct a formal, annual evaluation of the CEO's performance.
- Opportunity to devote time to the company's long-term strategy and to identify the potential risks to the firm.

*—Jay A. Conger, Edward E. Lawler III, and
David L. Finegold,* Corporate Boards: New
Strategies for Adding Value at the Top *(2001)*

What is worth doing is worth the trouble of asking somebody to do it.

—Ambrose Bierce, The Devil's Dictionary *(1906)*

But the vision of the Free Market has its dark side. Many of those who endow market capitalism with almost magical powers are well aware of it but accept it as a piece of progress. The late economist Joseph Schumpeter, a strong supporter of free-market capitalism, underscored capitalism's power of "creative destruction"; its tendency to act as an uncontrollable force of nature impersonal, implacable and in the short run radically disruptive of jobs, skills and older enterprises. For those who succeed in riding the back of the tiger, the capitalism of the free market is wonderful. But it holds less appeal for those who fall in the path of its creative destruction.

—*Daniel Yankelovich,* The Magic of Dialogue *(1999)*

First ask yourself: What is the worst that can happen? Then prepare to accept it. Then proceed to improve on the worst.

—*Dale Carnegie (1888–1955)*

"M" stands for making money for others and helping others make money. Helping others make money and helping other people to fulfill their desires is a sure way to ensure you'll make money for yourself as well as more easily fulfill your own dreams.

—*Deepak Chopra,* Creating Affluence *(1993)*

People often resort to job politics because they feel that the organization does not fairly judge their suitability for promotion. Similarly, when management has no objective way of differentiating effective from less effective employees, they will resort to favoritism. The adage, "It's not what you know but whom you know," applies accurately to organizations that lack clear-cut standards of performance.

—*Andrew J. DuBrin,* Winning Office Politics *(1990)*

I do not like charity cases. I believe my operations should have the sense of security that comes from knowing their work leads to a profit.

—*S. I. Newhouse, in* What Would Machiavelli Do?
by Stanley Bing (2000)

Anyone who has never made a mistake has never tried anything new.

—*Albert Einstein (1879–1955)*

I follow six clear-cut rules that represent the foundations of fairness, respect, and trust, rules that I believe have contributed to our . . . world championships:
- I treat team players with honesty and trust, and ask for the same in return.
- I make an unstated agreement with each team player: "Give me effort and I'll never second-guess you. I'll always defend you."
- I apply rules evenhandedly to all team members.
- I never air grievances to others, including the media, before I privately air my grievance with a player.
- I never humiliate or embarrass a team player in front of others.
- I don't play favorites. I offer no special favors to high-salaried stars or players I like, nor do I make a show of personal preferences.

—*Joe Torre, manager of the New York Yankees,*
Joe Torre's Ground Rules for Winners
with Harry Dreher (1999)

Failure is the only opportunity to begin again more intelligently.
—Henry Ford (1863–1947), founder of the Ford Motor Company

Our insurance premiums went up slightly when we decided to provide [all our employees] with full coverage. But that was offset by the lower attrition rate. We normally spend 25 hours of classroom training on every new employee. The longer an employee stays with us, the more we save.

—Howard Schultz, founder and CEO of the coffee bar chain Starbucks, in Inc. *(1993)*

If you dream of making a profit, you are being cautioned to keep your private affairs to yourself for the next few weeks and to avoid being drawn into the personal affairs of others.

—Lady Stearn Robinson and Tom Corbett,
The Dreamers Dictionary *(1974)*

The Jimmy Stewart S&L's are my favorite. They've quietly been making a profit all along. These are the no-frills, low-cost operators who take in deposits from the neighborhood and are content to make old-fashioned residential mortgage loans. They can be found in small cities and towns across America and in certain urban areas the commercial banks have overlooked. Many have big branches with enormous deposit bases, which are much more profitable than having a lot of tiny branches.

—Peter Lynch, Beating the Street *(1994)*

In sum, we feel that boards today need to define their shareholders more broadly. Whereas the 1980s and 1990s were the era of the shareholders, the twenty-first century needs to be characterized by a broader stakeholder model if governance models are to match the needs of the global economy and society. Our narrow conception of shareholders as the investors in a company does not reflect today's reality. Employees and suppliers are also making highly specialized, at-risk investments in firms. In a knowledge-based economy these investments can be thought of as equal in significance to the equity that is purchased by stockholders. Corporate boardrooms must reflect this new world of multiple "investors" if directors are to truly lead their corporations into the future.

—Jay A. Conger, Edward E. Lawler III, and David L. Finegold, Corporate Boards: New Strategies for Adding Value at the Top *(2001)*

CEOs have this obsession to know everything and control everything. I mean that's stupid.

—Ed McCracken, founder and CEO of Silicon Graphics, in In the Company of Giants *by Rama Dev Jager and Rafael Orti (1997)*

Managing Your Boss:
According to writer Marie-Jeanne Julliand, there are five key ways to manage your boss:
1. Offer solutions not complaints. Whining about a problem or blaming someone else for it puts your boss on the defensive. . . .
2. Apologize. If you make a mistake admit you are wrong. . . .

3. Stay central in the information flow. Make a point of being up-to-date in the areas for which your boss needs information.
4. Praise your boss. Giving genuine compliments can reap surprising rewards.
5. Build alliances. Other managers in the organization may be able to serve as mentors and give you valuable information on how to approach your boss.

—*Bob Nelson,* 1,001 Ways to Take the Initiative at Work *(1999)*

Of all the newly appointed CEOs, roughly 10 percent are fired, with half of them failing within the first three years.

—*Professor Richard F. Vancic of the Harvard Business School, in* Fortune *(1988)*

When it is not necessary to change, it is necessary not to change.

—*Lucius Cary, Viscount Falkland (1610–1643)*

The world hates change, yet it is the only thing that has brought progress.

—*Charles F. Kettering (1876–1958)*

It's easy to get sucked away from running the company. Politicians come knocking on the door; donations are sought from charities you never heard of; friends you've forgotten about come out of the woodwork; former adversaries become intimates.

—*Allen Michaels, CEO of Convergent Technologies, in* Time *magazine (1984)*

By design the "B-School" trains a senior officer class, the nonplaying captains of industry. . . . This elite, in my opinion, is missing some pretty fundamental requirements for success: humility; respect for people on the firing line; deep understanding of the nature of the business and the kind of people who can enjoy themselves making it prosper; respect from way down the line; a demonstrated record of guts in industry, judgment, fairness and honesty under pressure.

—Robert Townsend, Up the Organization *(1970)*

When Frank's in a meeting, the whole chemistry changes. People are waiting for his signals. What he really wants is reaction and debate. But what he often gets are people playing the situation, thinking, "What does Frank want?" And once they see which way he is leaning, a couple of people will hop on it and the train is rolling.

—Former colleague of Frank Lorenzo, then the CEO of Texas Air, who went on to bankrupt Eastern and Continental Airlines, in Business Week *(1987)*

One of our senior managers had a meeting with his staff to discuss work-life balance. The meeting started at five P.M. and ended at nine—and the manager didn't see the irony.

—Lewis E. Platt, CEO of Hewlett-Packard (1995)

When you see executives who get too hung up on perquisites like private airplanes or executive dining rooms or private washrooms, you've got to question what they're really focusing on.

—Chuck Ames of the buyout firm Clayton, Dublier & Rice, in The New York Times *(1993)*

When things go bad, cut the pay at the top first. When things go well, reward the bottom first.

—*Steve Ashton, CEO of Ashton Photo, Inc. (1994)*

Cost, cost, cost. Service, service, service. People, people, people. The business model is understandable by any three-year-old.

—*Tom Peters, management guru, on the management style at Southwest Airlines, in* The New York Times Magazine *(1997)*

Just as the student now feels technique is more important than content, so the trainee believes managing is an end in itself, an expertise relatively independent of the content of what is being managed.

—*William H. Whyte,* The Organization Man *(1956)*

Even as a manager you have to add value. You have to be good at something in the area you're working in. You can't just say, "Well, I am a manager so I will just manage and coordinate these people." People don't require that kind of management anymore.

—*Vinod Dhan, employee of Intel, in* Fortune *(1994)*

The largest American corporations grant their executives the privileges of infants. The company provides expense allowances, medical treatment, trips and entertainment, planes, picnics and outings, cars, club memberships and above all else, a ferociously protective secretary who, like a good English nanny, arranges the daily schedule, pays the bills, remembers to send flowers for anniversaries and holidays, makes dinner reservations and invents excuses that the nice gentleman's creditors or mistress might find plausible. The comforts and conveniences supposedly permit the executives to do a better job; in fact, they encourage the habit of infantilism prevalent at the higher altitudes of corporate privilege.

—*Lewis H. Lapham,* Money and Class in America *(1988)*

The job for big companies, the challenge that we all face as bureaucrats, is to create the environment where people can reach their dreams—and they don't have to do it in a garage.

—*Jack Welch, CEO of General Electric,* in Fortune *(1995)*

There is a wide gap between the number of executives who are street smart and the number of executives who think they are. Those who account for this numerical discrepancy are often found languishing in middle and lower-middle management, usually blaming anything and anybody but themselves for their lack of advancement. . . . But their instincts are bad. What they pick up perceptively they always manage to misuse. Deep down inside they know what should or should not be said and where or when to say it, but they can't help themselves. They blurt out some indiscretion, or don't check their need to "tell it like it is," even when they are aware that it is in their own worst interest to do so. This of course is business immaturity, and it afflicts as many people in their forties and fifties as it does in their twenties and thirties.

—*Mark McCormack,* What They Don't Teach
You at Harvard Business School *(1984)*

It is common sense to take a method and try it. If it fails, admit it freely and try another. But above all, try something.

—*Franklin D. Roosevelt (1882–1945), the only four-term
president of the United States*

Tired people make bad decisions. That's what Ronald Reagan told me.

—*Dick Jenrette, cofounder of Donaldson Lufken Jenrette
and former CEO of Equitable, in* Fortune *(1996)*

A decision is what a man makes when he can't get anyone to serve on a committee.

—*Fletcher Knebel, American novelist*

This is a basic and simple business. People create problems by not trusting their own judgment. By creating a committee. By constantly needing validation, you guys are empowered. You can find 99 percent of the answer in the aisles, where the customers are.

—*Bernie Marcus, cofounder and CEO of
Home Depot, in* Fortune *(1996)*

Being aggressive is a lot less risky in the end. Are you going to eat lunch, or have your lunch eaten for you?

—*William T. Esrey, CEO of Sprint, in* The New York Times *(1992)*

Leaders have powerful enemies. There's a war going on out there, and it is not for the faint of heart. The good guys do not always win.

—*Patricia Pitcher,* The Drama of Leadership *(1997)*

You must have clear goals
Give yourself a clear agenda
Let people know where they stand
What's broken, fix now
No repainting the flagpole
Lay the concept out, but let your people execute it
Never lie, ever
When in charge, take command
Do what's right

—*General Norman Schwartzkopf's rules for leaders, in* Inc. *(1992)*

The chairman of the board still needs his "attaboys"—perhaps more than anybody—but once you're on the top rung there are no more superiors to pat you on the back. This is the paradox of power. The more you have, the more vulnerable you feel to being exploited.

—*Jay B. Rorhlich, Wall Street psychiatrist, in* Forbes *(1985)*

You are being judged internally over the long haul. This places less of a premium on calculation and more on developing an ongoing support system of friends and allies. You can make a mentor outside the company with a few well-placed phone calls and occasional well-timed get-togethers. Mentorism inside the company is a week-in, week-out, month-to-month proposition. . . .

Within the company, you are also more likely to be "found out." Your real self is likely to emerge, and your weaknesses as well as your strengths are likely to be discovered. As a result, you must realize that "you get along by going along."

—*Mark McCormack,* What They Don't Teach
You at Harvard Business School *(1984)*

One of the hardest tasks of leadership is understanding that you are not what you are, but what you're perceived to be by others.

—*Edward L. Flom, CEO of the Florida Steel Corporation (1987)*

The price you pay for conformity is lack of creativity.

—*Timothy Price of MCI communications, in* Business Week *(1994)*

If you get into the hearts and minds of employees, they will buy the truth. Dialogue is the oxygen of change.

—*Jim MacLachlin of the accounting and consulting
firm Deloitte & Touche, in* Fortune *(1996)*

I think consensus is a poor substitute for leadership. Many CEOs are impeccably logical, but they don't lift your heart. They rely too much on the way things should be done. I believe in provocative disruption.

—*Charlotte Beers, CEO of the ad agency
Ogilvy & Mather, in* Fortune *(1996)*

Too often a layoff is viewed as some sort of virile gesture, a way of saying that senior management is hard-minded and serious.

—Frederick Reichold of the management consulting firm Bain & Co., in Fortune *(1996)*

A lot of people who call themselves leaders just slow things down. They're insecure, or don't believe in delegation, or aren't willing to deal with the arteriosclerosis that's weakening their organization. By the time they get to be CEOs, many leaders lose their appetite for dealing with change.

—Michael Walsh, former CEO of Tenneco, in Fortune *(1993)*

I bring my board my toughest problems, not my easiest. I don't want a paperwork board, but one that thinks like owners.

—Paul O'Neill, former CEO of the aluminum company Alcoa, in Fortune *(1993)*

The key themes in "Reinventing the Corporation" can be distilled into a checklist of questions to help you measure a company where you work, or are considering working:
- Is this a company where I will experience personal growth?
- Does this company reward performance and initiative or is everyone treated the same?
- What is the vision of this company?
- How is this company structured?
- Where does the company stand on health and fitness?
- Is this company flexible about job arrangements or is it strictly a 9 to 5 operation?

- How successful have women been in this company?
- Is this company involved in programs with local schools?
- Is this company thinking about lifelong training and education?
- Is this a company where people are having fun?

—John Naisbitt and Patricia Aburdene,
Reinventing the Corporation *(1985)*

Sometimes when I walk in my sons' and son-in-law's offices—they are all on the same floor as mine—I hear their cackling and laughter—you never used to hear that. Before, when you worked for Ingram, you were serious. I don't fault Bronson's style, but I can't work that way. I have a different style and that maybe is the result of having had a family. I want my children to be happy and have a good time and I think this attitude has permeated throughout the company. I think a sense of fun can be good. People became more productive. They have a sense that it's okay to be jolly.

—Martha R. Ingram, widow and successor of Bronson
Ingram as CEO of Ingram Industries, in Lessons
from the Top *by Thomas J. Neff and James M. Citrin*
with Paul B. Brown (2001)

A few yes-men may be born, but mostly they are made. Fear is a great breeder of them. An employer who habitually makes yes-men is a poor sort to be associated with. He doesn't develop men's abilities, likes only his ideas, is stingy with praise and cash, rules by fear, makes less money than he might.

—William J. Wrigley Jr., founder of the Wrigley Comany,
in In the Words of Great Business Leaders
by Julie M. Fenster (2000)

First, I think you really have to know the business. I am not so sure that these hired guns who come in to run one kind of business for a couple of years, and then go off to run another, are effective long term. I am assuming that by the time somebody's even a candidate for a top-level position he has experience and brains. Given all that, I look at whether the candidate's management style and the culture of the company he is going to help run are a good match. An autocratic style that might work in one industry or company could really blow up in another. This style thing cannot go unnoticed. When you factor everything else out, it may be the most important thing.

—*Carol Bartz, CEO of Autodesk, Inc., in*
Lessons from the Top *by Thomas J. Neff and James M. Citrin with Paul B. Brown (2001)*

LEADERSHIP

To be reasonably effective it is not enough for the individual to work hard or to be knowledgeable. Effectiveness is something separate, something different. But to be effective also does not require special gifts, special aptitude, or special training. Effectiveness as an executive demands doing certain—and fairly simple—things. It consists of a small number of practices. . . . All the effective ones (executives I have met in forty-five years of work) have had to learn to be effective. And all of them have had to practice effectiveness until it became a habit.

—*Peter Drucker,* The Effective Executive *(1999)*

The great accomplishments of man have resulted from the transmission of ideas and enthusiasm.

—*Thomas J. Watson, former chairman of IBM, in* The Forbes Book of Business Quotations, *edited by Ted Goodman (1997)*

The aim of leadership is to help others to achieve their personal bests. This involves setting high but realistic performance goals for yourself and your staff, finding ways to improve operations and procedures, and striving for total quality in all areas.

- Always strive to preach quality and practice improvement.
- Ensure that you involve all staff members in quality-improving programs.
- Promotion to leadership positions used to depend on rising up the company hierarchy. Now, vital work is increasingly carried out by temporary teams working on specific projects, which provide ideal opportunities for learning leadership skills.
- Use projects as a way of learning more about other disciplines.
- Make friends with people in different departments, and get to know how they operate.

—*Robert Heller,* Learning to Lead *(1999)*

In the first half of the 1980s, we restructured this company and changed its physical makeup. That was the easy part. In the last several years, our challenge has been to change ourselves, an infinitely more difficult task that, frankly, not all of us in leadership positions are capable of. . . .

—*Jack Welch, CEO of General Electric, in*
Jack Welch Speaks *by Janet Lowe (1998)*

The three great essentials to achieve anything worthwhile are first, hard work; second, stick-to-itiveness; and third, common sense.

—*Thomas Edison, in* The Forbes Book of Business
Quotations, *edited by Ted Goodman (1997)*

But if the superior recognizes the existence of the intricate interdependent characteristic of modern industry, and if he is less interested in personal power than in creating conditions such that the human resources available to him will be utilized to achieve organizational purposes, he will seek to build a strong group. He will recognize that the highest commitment to organizational objectives and the most successful collaboration in achieving them require unique kinds of interactions which can only occur in a highly effective group setting. He will in fact discourage discussion or decision-making on many matters which affect his organization except in a group setting. He will give the idea of "the team" full expression, with all the connotation it carries on the football field.

—*Douglas McGregor,* The Human Side of Enterprise *(1960)*

The key to an effective mentoring program is to choose people who are temperamentally suited to the task. They don't necessarily need to be your most senior managers. They should, however, be naturally empathetic and enjoy the role of helping others. Following are some suggestions on how to find those people in the company best suited to fill the role:

- Get recommendations. Ask your managers to recommend members of their own staffs who have the personality— and the workload—to act as effective mentors. Make sure that whomever they recommend has the time to devote to the task.

- Find common ground. Look for things—same school, similar hobbies—that can create a rapport between the mentor and the new employee.

- Choose good role models. Pick employees whose attitudes you'd really want the new employee to emulate.

- Provide training. If they've never mentored before, make sure that employees you ask to assume this role understand what you expect of them and what they can expect.
- Emphasize the fine line between being positive and "hovering."

—*Max Messmer,* Human Resources Kit for Dummies *(1999)*

No one has ever met my expectations, with the exception of my wife.

—*Lou Gerstner, chairman of IBM, in* What Would Machiavelli Do? *by Stanley Bing (2000)*

The robber barons of post–Civil War America were also jungle fighters who rationalized their exploitation of people and resources under the ideology of social Darwinism and progress—new technology, railroad, industry, open land, immigration, and education. An example of one of the most intelligent, subtle, and complex of these entrepreneurial jungle fighters was Andrew Carnegie. . . .

The modern gamesman is best defined as a person who loves change and wants to influence its course. He likes to take calculated risks and is fascinated by technique and new methods. He sees a developing project, human relations, and his own career in terms of options and possibilities, as if they were a game. . . . His main goal is to be known as a winner, and his deepest fear is to be labeled a loser. . . .

Being tough in this sense is necessary to become a winner. Perhaps another reason why executives become tough and even subtly sadistic is because they have to accept constant humiliations. Their toughness is self-protective and their controlled meanness is a form of compensation to reassure themselves that they have not been totally emasculated by the corporation.

—*Michael Maccoby,* The Gamesman *(1976)*

The key to activating the laws of success is for you to become perfectly clear about what it is you want and exactly what it will look like when you have achieved it. Just as you wouldn't attempt to build a house without a plan, you wouldn't think of building a great life without a clear list of the goals you wish to attain and a written plan of action for the attainment of those goals.

—*Brian Tracy,* The 100 Absolutely Unbreakable Laws of Business Success *(2000)*

A good leader is first a good subordinate.

A leader must be decisive—his decisions a fulfillment of his duty, vision, and experience.

A good leader is humble. He guards against ego distorting his vision. . . .

A leader focuses his subordinates on their common goal and inspires them by his own devotion to achieving it.

A leader orders hard work and enforces necessary discipline but doesn't suffocate his subordinates' initiative or spirit.

—*H. W. Crocker III,* Robert E. Lee on Leadership *(2000)*

Success is best achieved when you are clear about the goal but flexible about the process of getting there. . . . How you can apply this law immediately:

Identify your most cherished assumptions in the most important areas of your business and personal life. What if they were wrong? What would you do differently from what you are doing today? What are your options?

List the five worst things that could happen in your personal or business life in the next year. What would you do if one or more of them occurred? Make a list of options for each emergency and begin thinking about alternate courses of action to the most important things you are dealing with today.

—*Brian Tracy,* The 100 Absolutely Unbreakable
Laws of Business Success *(2000)*

I always prefer to believe the best of everybody—it saves so much trouble.

—*Rudyard Kipling (1865–1936)*

. . . leaders acting—as well as caring, inspiring and persuading others to act—for certain shared goals that represent the values—the wants and needs, the aspirations and expectations—of themselves and the people they represent.

—*James McGregor Burns, historian, in* Robert E. Lee
on Leadership *by H. W. Crocker III (2000)*

People do not lack strength; they lack will.

—*Victor Hugo (1802–1885)*

If you don't believe that you have a destiny yet, you'd better get busy. There are many you can choose. Like:

I'm up from the depths. I came out of nowhere. I'm going someplace big, Ma!

I may be quiet and studious but underneath it all I'm a killer destined to dominate others with the speed and power of my intellect.

God has selected me for important work. His will be done.

Of all the most evil things that walk this world, I am the worst, and am destined to be their ruler.

I'm gonna be a big rock 'n' roll star.

—*Stanley Bing,* What Would Machiavelli Do? *(2000)*

Strength does not come from physical capacity. It comes from an indomitable will.

—*Mahatma Ghandi (1869–1948)*

I attribute Intel's ability to sustain success to being constantly on the alert for threats, either technological or competitive in nature. The word *paranoia* is meant to suggest that attitude, an attitude that constantly looks over the horizon for threats to your success.

—*Andy Grove, chairman of Intel, in* What Would
Machiavelli Do? *by Stanley Bing (2000)*

Natural Born Leaders:
- Many of us have leadership skills and don't know it. Leadership is based partly on personality, and partly on the twelve keys, including trust, respect, fairness, serenity, optimism, communication, and steadiness.

- Ask yourself who in your work life—or among family, friends or teachers—strikes you as being a great leader. Observe how they go about their business, and put your finger on what makes them inspiring.
- Be humble enough to learn about leadership from the leaders in your midst.

—Joe Torre, manager of the New York Yankees, Joe Torre's Ground Rules for Winners *with Henry Dreher (1999)*

I've yelled at people and I'm not ashamed of it. We have to run this company efficiently and without a bunch of babies who say, "Mommy yelled at me today." It's impossible to run a leveraged operation like camp. If you don't like it, leave.

—Linda Wachner, former CEO of Warnaco, in What Would Machiavelli Do? *by Stanley Bing (2000)*

The awareness of the ambiguity of one's achievements (as well as one's deepest failures) is a definite symptom of maturity.

—Paul Tillich, in The Forbes Book of Business Quotations, *edited by Ted Goodman (1997)*

As leader you should concentrate your time on activities that nobody else can do. Delegation is a form of time management. It is a way of exercising control and meeting your own responsibilities more effectively, while developing the skills of your staff.

- Remember that delegation boosts morale and builds confidence.
- Never keep work simply because you do it better.
- Set high targets in agreement with your delegates.

- If time pressure increases, ask if you are delegating enough to others.
- Check regularly and informally on progress of delegated tasks.
- Keep an open door for all your delegates.
- Intervene fast when the delegate cannot cope.
- Make sure everybody knows what must always be left to you.

—Robert Heller, Learning to Lead *(1999)*

The significance of man is not what he attains, but rather what he longs to attain.

—Khalil Gibran (1883–1931)

It is faddish to think of leaders as people who master competencies and emanate character. Leaders do much more than demonstrate character.... Effective leaders get results.

—David Ulrich, Jack Zenger, and Norm Smallwood,
Results-Based Leadership *(1999)*

There are lots of different characteristics that can make somebody a success. I think it is important as a leader to play to your strengths and not try to be somebody that you're not. My strength is involvement. People know that I am going to be there for them and also know that I am going to be on top of the details.

—Sanford I. Weill, chairman and CEO of Citigroup, Inc.,
in Lessons from the Top *by Thomas J. Neff and*
James M. Citrin with Paul B. Brown (2001)

The farther we keep away from the "boss" proposition—of being the "boss" of the men under us—the more successful we are going to be. If a man cannot be a real assistant and furnish assistance to the men under him then he has no business being over them at all. That is not one of our problems [at IBM], but it does exist in many places throughout the country, where a man, because of his impressive title, assumes the attitude of a "boss" and tells people what to do, instead of helping them do it.

—*Thomas J. Watson Sr., founder of IBM, in*
In the Words of Great Business Leaders
by Julie M. Fenster (2000)

What I'm talking about is self-invention. Imagination. That's basically how we get to know ourselves. People who cannot invent and reinvent themselves must be content with borrowed postures, secondhand ideas, and "fitting in" instead of "standing out."

—*Warren Bennis, "An Invented Life" in*
The Encyclopedia of Leadership
by Murray Hiebert and Bruce Klatt (2001)

Be ye ensured that I will be as good unto you as ever a Queen was unto her people. No will in me can lack, neither do I trust shall there lack any power. And persuade yourselves that for the safety and quietness of you all will not spare if I need be to spend my blood.

—*Elizabeth I, from an address prior to her coronation as queen of England (1558)*

HUMAN RESOURCES

In this (global and diverse) business environment, your career success depends on your ability to work effectively with co-workers and customers who are different from you. Research has shown that companies that embrace diversity produce more, experience lower turnover, relate better to a wider range of customers, and make more money. These companies look for employees who respect and value differences, appreciate new ideas and ways of thinking, and search for methods to capitalize on everyone's diverse strengths.

—*Beverly Rokes,* Quick Skills: Embracing Diversity *(2001)*

First there was the Protestant ethic—we work happily for the glory of God—which grew out of the predestination of Calvinism and the individualism and asceticism of the Quakers. That was secularized by Benjamin Franklin, among others, into what's called the craft ethic; we work diligently for ourselves. It made a great deal of sense in a nation where 80 percent of the population were self-employed farmers and craftsmen. As Franklin said, "God helps those who help themselves."

In the new world, a world in which there's no such thing as corporate loyalty, a world where young people graduating from good colleges can land positions only as temps, a world where raises are rare and barely keep pace with the cost of living, viewing yourself and your job as one is dangerous psychologically and financially. The answer is to quit today: mentally separate yourself from your employer and realize that you're on your own. . . . Once you've quit in your head, being fired is no longer a real threat: you're already a free agent on the lookout for your next opportunity.

—Stephen M. Pollan and Mark Levine, Die Broke *(1997)*

The whole life of an American is passed like a game of chance. A revolutionary crisis, or a battle. As the same causes are continually in operation throughout the country, they ultimately impart an irresistible impulse to the national character.

—Alexis de Tocqueville, Democracy in America *(1835)*

They are not the workers, nor are they the white-collar people in the usual, clerk sense of the word. These people only work for The Organization. The ones I am talking about belong to it as well. They are the ones of our middle class who have left home, spiritually, as well as physically, to take the vows of organizational life, and it is they who are the mind and soul of our great self-perpetuating institutions. Only a few are top managers or ever will be. In a system that makes such hazy terminology as "junior executive" psychologically necessary, they are staff as well as line and most are destined to live poised in a middle area that still awaits a satisfactory euphemism. But they are the dominant members of our society nonetheless.

—*William H. Whyte Jr.,* The Organization Man *(1956)*

Welcome to the number-one challenge that you face in the decade ahead: managing change. And the number-one contribution that you can make in the HR realm is to become a true catalyst for change in your organization. You must, therefore, be able not only to envision the kinds of changes, structural and otherwise, that your company must make to meet the challenges of the future, but also to persuade senior management to adopt those changes. And you also need to be the one who gets all your company's line managers up to speed on all the HR practices that you must set into place if your company's to keep pace with change. . . .

The "human" side of work experience is no longer an issue that companies can afford to take for granted. And that's why the human resources function itself has begun to assume so much more business importance. People responsible for the human resources function in progressive companies today are no longer viewed merely as "personnel administrators," and the roles they now play in operations are no longer viewed strictly as "support." Senior management increasingly calls on human resources specialists to help formulate long-term staffing strategies and to introduce and follow through on practices that help ensure that employees get the support and training they need to meet the ever-increasing demands of their jobs.

—*Max Messmer,* Human Resources Kit for Dummies *(1999)*

The key to an effective and useful résumé is very simple: you must know why you are writing it (to open doors for you, to help people remember you after you've interviewed with them, or both), to whom you are writing it (the man who has the power to hire), what you want him to know about you and how you can help him and his organization, and how you can support this claim so as to convince him to reach a favorable decision. You must know your primary functional goal (your strongest skill), plus your primary organizational goal (where you can do it best).

—*Richard Nelson Bolles,*
What Color Is Your Parachute? *(1972)*

To my mind, flextime is the essence of respect for and trust in people. It says that we both appreciate that our people have busy personal lives and that we trust them to devise, with their supervisor and work group, a schedule that is personally convenient yet fair to others.

—*David Packard, cofounder of Hewlett-Packard,*
The Hewlett-Packard Way *(1995)*

Don't be needlessly cruel in firing someone. Figure out a reason that is true but enables him to preserve ego. It is usually true that this combination of skills is not what's needed, or that the job is being restructured. If you don't feel compelled to destroy his self-regard, he can move on quickly and without scars.

—Robert Townsend, Up the Organization *(1970)*

For a team to work well, several roles must be played—not independently, but collectively. The leader's role is to develop a team that thinks and acts together, with individual and team interests aligned.

- Ensure that team members share the same goals.
- Encourage competition between ideas, not individuals.
- Boost a team's effectiveness by training members in new skills.
- Ask people if they have enough responsibility.
- Do not accept the opinions of others on team abilities.
- Allow new people and teams to prove how good they are.
- Reward real merit openly, but never appear to play any favorites.

—Robert Heller, Learning to Lead *(1999)*

First of all he usually gives me the reprimand as soon as I've done something wrong. Second, since he specifies exactly what I did wrong, I know he is "on top of things" and that I'm not going to get away with sloppiness. Third, since he doesn't attack me as a person—only my behavior—it's easier for me not to become defensive. I don't try to rationalize away my mistake by fixing blame on him or somebody else. I know he is being fair. And fourth, he is consistent.

—Ms. Brown describing her boss, "The One Minute Manager," in The One Minute Manager *by Kenneth Blanchard, Ph.D., and Spencer Johnson, M.D. (1981)*

There's a happening going on that I call "loss of accumulated wisdom." American companies are very busy now weeding out those older employees with twenty or thirty years' service. But what happens when they stop rearranging personnel and go back to running the business? The dialogue will go something like: "Well, how did we do this?" "I don't know; Harry always used to handle it when he was inventory control manager." "So, where the hell is Harry?" "He's the one we let go on the early retirement program." Those things catch up and affect the character of a particular business. The wisdom being lost now is eventually going to hurt our corporations.

—Peter N. Rogers, president and CEO of E.J. Brach Corporation,
in The Popcorn Report *by Faith Popcorn (1991)*

I have always felt that you shouldn't have to change your personality when you come to work. So we decided we are going to hire good people, and let them be themselves, let them be individualistic. We are going to create an environment where we pay a great deal of attention to them, their personal lives as well as their business lives. We wanted to show them that we don't regard them just as work automatons. We wanted to create an environment where people can really enjoy what they're doing.

—Herb Kelleher, founder and CEO of Southwest Airlines,
in Lessons from the Top *by Thomas J. Neff and*
James M. Citrin with Paul B. Brown (2001)

In private matters everyone is equal before the law. In public matters, when it is a question of putting power and responsibility into the hands of one man rather than another, what counts is not rank or money, but the ability to do the job well.

—*Pericles (ca. 495–429 B.C.)*

The first spiritual law of success is the law of pure potentiality. This law is based on the fact that we are, in our essential state, pure consciousness. Pure consciousness is our spiritual essence. Being infinite and unbounded, it is also pure joy . . . when you discover your essential nature and know who you really are, in that knowing itself is the ability to fulfill any dreams you have, because you are the eternal possibility, the immeasurable potential of all that was, is, and will be.

—*Deepak Chopra,* The Seven Spiritual Laws of Success *(1994)*

CAREERS

Careerism results not only in constant anxiety, but also in an underdeveloped heart. Overly concerned with adapting himself to others, to marketing himself, the careerist constantly betrays himself, since he must ignore idealistic, compassionate, and courageous impulses that might jeopardize his career. As a result, he never develops an inner center, a strong independent sense of self, and eventually he loses touch with his deepest strivings. . . . Erich Fromm has analyzed careerism in terms of the "marketing orientation," pointing out that the individual's sense of identity, integrity, and self-determination is lost when he treats himself as an object whose worth is determined by its fluctuating market value.

—Michael Maccoby,
The Gamesman *(1976)*

Every man's work shall be made manifest: for the day shall declare it, because it shall be revealed by fire; and the fire shall try every man's work or what sort it is.

—*I Corinthians 3:13*

If you think you can, you can; if you think you can't, you're right.

—*Mary Kay Ash, founder of Mary Kay Cosmetics,
in* A Woman's Way to Incredible Success in
Business *by Mary-Ellen Drummond (2001)*

The corporate world is a stagnant, superficial, unsatisfying, dishonest, horrible environment. Why would anybody want to join it? The smart person is sitting back and re-evaluating all the options, saying I don't need this, and leaving. We'll be seeing a shift from manufacturing-driven businesses to service-oriented businesses. Entrepreneurs: your time is now.

—*Marquis Visich de Visoko, Knight-Grand Crosi,
in* The Popcorn Report *by Faith Popcorn (1991)*

Always try to work for the smartest, brightest, most competent person you can find. If you look at biographies of successful people, it's amazing to find how many crawled up the ladder of success right behind someone else. From their first assignment in some menial job to their last as president or CEO of a major company.

Yet some people actually like to work for incompetents. I suppose they feel that a fresh flower stands out better if it's surrounded by wilted ones. They forget the tendency of top management to throw the whole bunch out if they become dissatisfied with the operation.

—*Al Ries and Jack Trout,* Positioning *(2001)*

Know your limits, skills and potential:
- Recognize your own talents and skill sets.
- Stay within yourself—know your limits—but realize that within those bounds your potential is limitless.
- Remember that knowledge of your own strengths combined with maximum effort to improve yields a formula for success. . . .

When you must release an employee, I recommend these guidelines, under the "get issues out on the table" category.
- Whenever possible, break the news yourself.
- Be straightforward and take responsibility for the decision. Don't put the blame on someone else, as in "I wanted to keep you, but he didn't."
- Thank the team player for his or her contributions.
- Don't break the news in a mechanical way because you feel bad about what you're doing. Show some compassion, because you know how you'd feel in his or her shoes.

—*Joe Torre, manager of the New York Yankees,*
Joe Torre's Ground Rules for Winners
with Harry Dreher (1999)

The jobs most people have existed before they got there and will continue to exist after they've left. The job is the constant. What you do by going beyond it is what gets noticed.

Most positions in a company are three-quarters functional, meaning the set responsibilities and duties that come with it, and one-quarter personal style. The degree by which you can stretch this 25 percent is the degree by which you will stand out in your company.

—*Mark McCormack,* What They Don't Teach
You at Harvard Business School *(1984)*

Least effort is expended when your actions are motivated by love, because nature is held together by the energy of love. When you seek power and control over people, you waste energy. When you seek money or power for the sake of ego, you spend energy chasing the illusion of happiness instead of enjoying happiness in the moment. When you seek money for personal gain only, you cut off the flow of energy to yourself and interfere with the expression of nature's intelligence. But when your actions are motivated by love, there is no waste of energy . . .

—*Deepak Chopra,* The Seven Spiritual
Laws of Success *(1994)*

Retreats are held in fabulous locations from Sanibel Island, Florida, to Palm Desert, California. The rooms are huge and cool. Golf is free. The food goes on for miles. Drinks are mandatory. Get your company to organize an "offsite" that you'll get invited to. Call it strategic planning. Man, that's living.

—*Stanley Bing,* What Would
Machiavelli Do? *(2000)*

The only way to definitely increase your job satisfaction and/or your income is to get another job. The more you move from job to job, the more likely you are to continually increase your income. The secret is for you to find a new job before they can fire you. That's why you should always be looking for a new job. . . .

In the new world, you need to learn four new but equally simple maxims:

1. Quit today
2. Pay cash
3. Don't retire
4. Die broke

Together these four simple axioms form a mantra for living in the new world.

—Stephen M. Pollan and Mark Levine, Die Broke *(1997)*

People who feel good about themselves produce good results.

—Kenneth Blanchard, Ph.D., and Spencer Johnson, M.D.,
The One Minute Manager *(1981)*

Women are realizing now that it's hard to be Super Woman. It isn't so great to double your family's income, if it means you have to turn your back on your family and your home.

—Martha Stewart, founder of Martha Stewart, Inc.,
in The Popcorn Report *by Faith Popcorn (1991)*

The Craft Ethic lasted more than a century. The Career Ethic lasted fifty years. And now, after only two decades, it's time to abandon the Self-Fulfillment Ethic and adopt what

I call the Mercantile Ethic. . . . I am simply urging you to abandon the single-minded pursuit of self-fulfillment through employment.

Perhaps it is this specter that most haunts working men and women: the planned obsolescence of people that is of a piece with the things they make. Or sell. It is perhaps this fear of no longer being needed in a world of needless things that most clearly spells out the unnaturalness, the surreality of much of what is called work today.

—*Studs Turkel,* Working *(1974)*

A firm's IQ is determined by the degree to which its infrastructure connects, shares and structures information. Isolated applications and data, no matter how impressive, can produce idiot savants but not a highly functional corporate behavior.

—*Bill Gates,* Business @ the Speed of Thought *(1999)*

The "work ethic" holds that labor is good in itself; that a man or woman becomes a better person by virtue of the act of working. America's competitive spirit, the "work ethic" of this people, is alive and well on Labor Day, 1971.

—*Richard Nixon (1913–1994)*

No matter how much different kinds of work may vary upon the surface, underneath they have this common base: they deal with one kind of problem-solving or another. Universities, community organizations, businesses—all require people good at problem-solving no matter what title may be tacked upon the man or woman they hire in order to justify his or her salary. Problem solvers get hired, whether they are fresh out of college, or later in life.

—*Richard Nelson Bolles,* What Color Is Your Parachute? *(1972)*

How people perceive you determines the way they react to what you say. How you communicate, or fail to communicate, will determine how others translate your thoughts and actions. This is especially true when cultural barriers limit the give-and-take of easy conversations. Your goal is to reduce any negative perceptions that may interfere with the conversations, meetings, presentations, or other interactions you have with individuals from cultures that are different from yours. . . .

Think about what your speech and body language communicate. Do they tend to convey equality or superiority, genuine interest or aloofness, acceptance or disdain? By communicating equality, interest, and acceptance, you will show your co-workers that you respect them.

—*Beverly Rokes,* Quick Skills: Embracing Diversity *(2001)*

You've got to get the right management—and that doesn't mean tweaking it a little here or a little there. . . . The people who have created a problem are not all of a sudden going to improve, so I get rid of almost all the senior management and bring in people who have worked with me before.

—*"Chain Saw" Al Dunlap, restructuring expert, on his rationale for cutting 50 percent of corporate staff and 20 percent of all employees at Lily Tulip, in* What Would Machiavelli Do? *by Stanley Bing (2000)*

As the automated pace of our daily jobs wipes out our name and face—and, in many instances, feelings—there is a sacrilegious question being asked these days. To earn one's bread by the sweat of one's brow has always been the lot of mankind. At least, ever since Eden's slothful couple was served with an eviction notice.

—*Studs Turkel,* Working *(1974)*

That is what we often do with new, inexperienced people. We welcome them aboard, take them around to meet everybody, and then we leave them alone. Not only do we not catch them doing anything approximately right, but periodically we zap them just to keep them moving. This is the most popular leadership style of all. We call it the "leave alone–zap" style. You leave a person alone, expecting good performance from them, and when you don't get it, you zap them. . . . And that's what's wrong with most businesses today.

—*Kenneth Blanchard, Ph.D., and Spencer Johnson, M.D.,*
The One Minute Manager *(1981)*

The key to success is to take new, objective, and creative approaches to encouraging beneficial change, rather than to repeat ourselves endlessly and negatively, as critics tend to do. When a person's performance is not up to standard they may need information rather than criticism.

—*Gordon F. Shea,* Mentoring *(1997)*

There are at least five sets of goals, which we may call basic needs. These are briefly physiological, safety, love, esteem, and self-actualization. In addition, we are motivated by the desire to achieve or maintain the various conditions upon which these basic satisfactions rest. . . . Thus man is a perpetually wanting animal. Ordinarily the satisfaction of all these wants is not altogether mutually exclusive, but only tends to be.

—Abraham H. Maslow, "The Hierarchy of Need"
in The Maslow Business Reader

As an employee, you must:
- Know your own skills, strengths and weaknesses;
- Put yourself in positions to succeed by finding ways to demonstrate your talents;
- Accept your assigned role by being professional, and by being willing to work diligently to fulfill your promise, even if you don't completely agree with your manager's decision.

—Joe Torre, manager of the New York Yankees,
Joe Torre's Ground Rules for Winners
with Harry Dreher (1999)

What Apple has really been to me is an opportunity to express some deep feeling about wanting to contribute meaning. I really believe that people have a desire to put something back, to give something in a greater way. . . . In a sense, that's part of the joy of Apple Computer. . . . [The company is] sort of a framework . . . where, if it's done right, people can really put something back.

—Steve Jobs, cofounder of Apple Computer, in
Clicks and Mortar: Passion Driven Growth in an
Internet Driven World *by David S. Pottruck*
and Terry Pearce (2000)

The biggest thing that has happened in the last decade is that no one now feels secure. You can't cut forty percent of a company and have the sixty percent remaining assume that they have a job for life. I think the Japanese will be feeling it next. Once that overextended economy starts laying people off, the concept of what Japan stands for—lifetime employment, loyalty to company—will be shattered.

—Jay Chiat, chairman and CEO worldwide of Chiat/Day/Mojo/Inc. Advertising, in The Popcorn Report *by Faith Popcorn (1991)*

Eventually it comes down to this: Are you good at what you do? If not, either become real good at it or find something else. There ought to be something in the world that you are good at. . . .

If you are talented, you can see opportunities where others see disasters.

—Dave Murphy, "Layoffs Looming? Act to Protect Yourself" in The San Francisco Chronicle *(2001)*

Despite its widespread appearance (people now think it's a fundamental part of the American Dream), retirement is a fairly new concept. It's an idea that worked for one generation only and that was because of a demographic fluke. Far from being a natural part of the life cycle, it's a form of social engineering—and an outdated one at that.

—Stephen M. Pollan and Mark Levine, Die Broke *(1997)*

THE WORKPLACE

Companies today are smaller, leaner, and not as hierarchically structured as they were as recently as 15 years ago. Most everybody knows about this particular change. But the most significant change in the organizational structure of most companies has less to do with the fundamental structure of companies and more to do with the fundamental nature of jobs—and the working arrangements of the people who hold the jobs.

—*Max Messmer,* Human Resources Kit for Dummies *(1999)*

The superior man is distressed by the limitations of his ability; he is not distressed by the fact that men do not recognize the ability he has.

—*Confucius (551–479 B.C.)*

Because your own strength is unequal to the task, do not assume that it is beyond the powers of man: but if anything is within the powers and province of man, believe that it is within your own compass also.

—Marcus Aurelius Antoninus (A.D. 121–180)

Neither talent without instruction nor instruction without talent can produce the perfect craftsman. He should be a man of letters, a skilled draughtsman, expert in geometry, not ignorant of optics, well grounded in arithmetic; he should know considerable history, have listened to philosophers diligently, should be acquainted with music; he should not be ignorant of medicine, he should be learned in the findings of the legal experts and should be familiar with astrology and the laws of astronomy.

—Vitruvius, (fl. 1st Century B.C.)

We owe to Smith [Adam Smith, author of *The Wealth of Nations*] the conception of the market economy as a self-regulating mechanism, harnessing as motive power the self-interest of participants, yet so integrating their activities that each is led to serve the desires of his fellows. . . . It is the fact of scarcity that forces us to make economic decisions, that is, to organize our efforts for production and/or to engage in trade with a view toward obtaining desired objects of consumption.

—Jack Hirshleifer and David Hirshleifer,
Price Theory and Applications *(1976)*

The only ideas that count are the A ideas. There is no second place. That means we have to get everyone in the organization involved. If you do that right, the best ideas will rise to the top.

—Jack Welch, CEO of General Electric,
in Jack Welch Speaks *by Janet Lowe (1998)*

Every new method, which leads by a shorter road to wealth, every machine that spares labor, every instrument that diminishes the cost of production, every discovery, which facilitates pleasures or augments them, seems to be the grandest effort of the human intellect.

—Alex de Tocqueville, Democracy in America *(1835)*

Who built the seven towers of Thebes?
The books are filled with the names of kings.
Was it kings who hauled the craggy blocks of stone? . . .
In the evening when the Chinese wall was finished
Where did the masons go?

—Bertolt Brecht (1898–1956)

[John D.] Rockefeller's golf was the exact reverse of Mr. Andrew Carnegie's golf. Carnegie could not stand being beaten and would take the utmost liberties with the score. Rockefeller was strictness itself in counting every stroke. I remember that one tee at Augusta faced a little swamp. If Rockefeller had the misfortune to drive into this morass, he would stop and put on a pair of rubbers, go into the mud and hammer at his ball. . . . Considering everything, he played a remarkable game, and always in strict conformity to the rules.

—*Frank Nelson Doubleday, founder of*
Doubleday & Company, Memoirs of a Publisher

He had to admit that the biggest inhibitor to change lies within yourself, and that nothing gets better until you change.

—*Spencer Johnson, M.D.,* Who Moved My Cheese? *(1998)*

When you don't have any money, the problem is food. When you have money, it's sex. When you have both, it's health.

—*J. P. Dunleavy,* The Ginger Man *(1955)*

It is often the people at the root of the company, on the shop floor, who will provide the best answers.

—*Hans Becherer, former CEO of the farm equipment*
firm Deere & Co., in Business Week *(1994)*

Joseph Scanlon, a steelworker and union organizer during the 1940s and 1950s, noticed that when labor and management cooperated and employees were part of the decision-making process, companies tended to be healthier and workers more productive. He devised the Scanlon Plan based on the principle of "organization development, identity, participation, and equity." . . .

In a recent online survey by iVillage.com, employees were asked, "What is the most important for getting ahead in the workplace?" Of the 7,760 people who cast their votes,

55 percent said that "initiative" is the most important, followed by "inspiration" (17 percent), "intelligence" (16 percent), and "political savvy" (12 percent). . . .

The biggest mistake in life is to think that you work for someone else. True, you may have a boss and you may collect a paycheck from a company but ultimately, you are a master of your own destiny. You decide what potential you reach in your career and what you will eventually accomplish in your life.

—*Bob Nelson,* 1,001 Ways to Take the Initiative at Work *(1999)*

Article 4 of the 1948 Universal Declaration of Human Rights guarantees that "no one shall be held in slavery or servitude, slavery and the slave trade shall be prohibited in all their forms." Yet slavery still occurs. Contemporary slaves still work in the fields, and provide manual labor for many industries in both rural and urban settings. Attempts to eradicate contemporary forms of slavery have been much less successful than the past century's campaigns against the traditional slave trade. Today's slaves include forced labor in Burma, child carpet weavers in Pakistan, bonded charcoal burners in Brazil, and bonded brick kiln workers in India.

—*Amy Domini,* Socially Responsible Investing *(2001)*

It is now clear that if present trends continue, by the turn of the century work forces in the United States, Australia, indeed throughout the industrial world, will increasingly stratify into two separate blocs. Fundamentally, people with high skills will earn high wages and people with low skills will earn low wages or no wages at all.

—*Lawrence Perlman, former CEO of the information and defense electronics firm Ceridian Corporation (1995)*

It is no doubt that the half-life of most job skills is dropping all the time.

—Edward Lawler, professor of management, University of South Carolina, in Time *magazine (1989)*

When the day comes that American Express Company has to hire a female employee, it will close its doors.

—James Congdell Fargo, president of American Express (1881–1914)

Women who are excitable and emotional may be dismissed as temperamentally unsuited for management. Yet men who vent their emotions by slamming the door and pounding the desk may be considered "aggressive." When I tell people I work for a bank, they almost always assume that I am a teller.

—Janet Martin, Canadian Imperial Bank of Commerce (1991)

I think the word "diversity" is divisive.

—Janet Hill, African-American management consultant, in Fortune *(1997)*

We don't want to be allowed in the men's locker room [of an all-male golf club], we just want to play golf.

—Jonina Jacobs, Detroit restaurateur, in Business Week *(1994)*

Top jobs are designed for people with wives.
—*Lucy Heller, employee of Booker, a British food company, in* The Economist, *(1992)*

Paul [Brown, the first National Football League owner to hire black players] was a top business person who was driven to setting up an organization that would be the best in the world, utilizing the best personnel, developing the best devices to win. Color never came into his philosophy—neither positive nor negative. The way he carried his organization was that everybody was afraid of him, so you didn't have any dissension.
—*Jim Brown, NFL Hall of Fame player and former running back for Paul Brown's Cleveland Browns, in* The New York Times *(1997)*

We're good at sending people to diversity training, using politically correct language, and making sure we have people of color in our Annual Report photos. But when it comes to the hard work of encouraging diversity—including new ways of thinking, implementing more flexible work schedules, or examining deep-rooted prejudices—we're much more reluctant. So while the surface problems get better and our workplace has all the outer trappings of diversity, the deep-seated issues of intolerance and exclusivity go unexamined.
—*Raymond W. Smith, chairman of Bell Atlantic (1993)*

It is no accident that the companies that practice affirmative action most conspicuously . . . are precisely those companies selling a product to consumers in the retail marketplace. Corporations are not inherently ideological, they are inherently greedy: if you will buy a product or service more readily from a minority, they will have minorities to pitch or sell their products.

—*Michael Lewis, in* The New York Times *(1996)*

If you don't have a workplace that reflects your customers, you are not going to be competitive.

—*Yvone Alverio, in* The Minority Career Guide
*by Michael E. Kastre, Nydia Rodriquez Kastre,
and Alfred G. Edwards (1993)*

Bill Gates probably has more to do, for good or ill, with the growth of productivity than Bill Clinton. Anyone who has spent time sitting in front of a computer screen, as we are doing, must frequently have felt that the new technology is a drag on productivity.

—*Herbert Stein, economist, in* Slate *(1996)*

The key question is do you want to take away the individual flexibility and freedom that the personal computer provides. People do play computer games at work but they also doodle with pencils. Do you take away their pencils? And the notion of telling workers they can go to this Web site, but not that one, is silly. That's not the way a modern work force is managed. You've got to trust people.

—*Bill Gates, chairman and cofounder of Microsoft,
in* The New York Times *(1996)*

The emotional contract with the employer has changed because people no longer see a job as being for life. Their loyalty now is not loyalty to the employer but to themselves, plus a desire to be professional in their work. We certainly tend not to go for people who are motivated only by money.

—*Dr. Paul Dorey of Barclay's Bank,*
in The Financial Times *(1997)*

Around here you're either expense or revenue.

—*Donna Vailluncourt, employee of the software*
firm Spectrum Associates, in Inc. *(1994)*

Suggestions for Intrapreneurs:
- Come to work each day willing to be fired.
- Ask for forgiveness rather than for permission.
- Do any task to make your dream work, regardless of your job description.
- Follow your intuition about people and build a team of the best.
- Work underground—publicity triggers the corporate immune system.
- Be true to your goals but be realistic about how to achieve them.
- Ask for advice before you ask for resources.
- Never bet on a race unless you are running in it.
- Keep the best interests of the company and its customers in mind, especially when you have to bend the rules or circumvent the bureaucracy.
- Honor and educate your sponsors.

—*Gifford Pichot, author of* Intrapreneuring,
in 1,001 Ways to Take the Initiative
at Work *by Bob Nelson (1999)*

Don't go into a dinner without a clear idea of what you want out of it. Otherwise, you could get played, instead of the other way around. . . . Always pick up the check. A little baby with a diaper and a bib has his food provided for him. A prince pays his own way.

—*Stanley Bing,* What Would Machiavelli Do? *(2000)*

When you're an athlete who's competed on a high level, people know you're a team player, willing to do what it takes to reach your goal. You build a certain amount of mental toughness, so even if you fail to guard that big account, you pick yourself up and go at it even harder next time.

—*Doug McNeely of the investment bank Donaldson, Lufkin & Jenrette and captain of the 1983 Duke University varsity basketball team, in* The New York Times *(1992)*

Most of us don't like to sit down and hear where we're lacking and where we need to improve. It's like sitting down with your mom and dad and they're telling you, "We know what's best."

—*An executive, in* The Wall Street Journal *(1996)*

There are cases where the job possesses the man even after quitting time. Aside from the occupational ticks of hourly workers and fitful sleep of salaried ones, there are instances of a man's singular preoccupation with work. It may affect his attitude toward all of life. And art.

—*Studs Turkel,* Working *(1974)*

Employees are very critical when wide gaps exist between [stated] values and actions. They watch to see how stated values are reinforced and how these values influence actions.

—*James Kouzes and Barry Posner,*
The Leadership Challenge *(1996)*

I don't really believe in, or pay much attention to, the folks who say that there's no work ethic in America today, because we get marvelous applicants all the time. But they are driven, they are motivated, they are inspired, by different things than people used to be. And so you have to be aware of that.

—*Herb Kelleher, founder and CEO of Southwest Airlines,*
in Lessons from the Top *by Thomas J. Neff and*
James M. Citrin with Paul B. Brown (2001)

And even though I've gotten to this position, I'm still running into yahoos every day who when we attend a meeting want me to run out and get everyone tea. That gets old. I don't try to pay a whole lot of attention to it, but you still get irritated. And then I say, gosh, if people are doing this to me, what the heck are they doing to women further down the organization?

—*Carol Bartz, CEO of Autodesk, Inc., in*
Lessons from the Top *by Thomas J. Neff and*
James M. Citrin with Paul B. Brown (2001)

Nothing is so much fun as business. I do not expect to do anything but work as long as I can stand up.

—*William J. Wrigley Jr., founder of the Wrigley Company,*
in In the Words of Great Business Leaders
by Julie M. Fenster (2000)

Women have always worked, but until the past century their work has been confined almost entirely to the domestic setting, and it has been for the most part unpaid labor. Women's work was an element in the larger family economy that predominated in preindustrial society. Although this work proved crucial to family subsistence, it also constituted the basis for women's subordinate position in patriarchal society. In the American colonies, for instance, women made substantial contributions to both agricultural production and domestic manufacture; still, married women could not own property, nor could they make contracts on their own. This legal framework reinforced the economic subordination of colonial women; without means for self-support, women's place was clearly in the home.

> —*Thomas Dublin,* Women at Work: The Transformation
> of Work and Community in Lowell, Massachusetts *(1979)*

FINANCE AND ACCOUNTING

Ultimately, marketing is the art of attracting and keeping profitable customers. Yet companies often discover that between 20 and 40 percent of their customers may be unprofitable. . . . A profitable customer is a person, household, or company that yields a revenue stream over time, exceeding by an acceptable amount the company cost stream of attracting, selling and servicing that customer. . . . Most companies fail to measure individual customer profitability.

—*Philip Kotler,* Marketing Management *(1994)*

Beware of little expenses. A small leak will sink a big ship.

—*Benjamin Franklin (1706–1790)*

Profit margin is an accounting term describing the ratio of a company's income to its sales. There are two types of profit margin: gross profit margin and net profit margin. Gross profit margin shows the percentage return that a company is earning over the cost of the merchandise sold. It is calculated by dividing gross profit, or sales, less cost of goods sold, by the total sales. Net profit margin, also called return on sales, shows the percentage of net income generated by each sales dollar. It is calculated by dividing the income statement figure for net income after taxes by total sales.

—Nitin Nohria, editorial director,
The Portable MBA Desk Reference *(1998)*

Annual reports are gold mines of information because they include the following financial statements and information:

Income Statement: Discloses all of the company's earnings and profits for the year.

Balance Sheet: Identifies all of the company's long- and short-term assets and liabilities.

Statement of Cash Flows: Tells you all the company's sources for and uses of cash for the past year.

Research and Development Expenses: Tells you a lot about where the company's headed in the future.

Overhead Expenses: High overhead expenses relative to total revenues can signal inefficient management or lagging markets for the company's products or services.

—Jill Gilbert, Getting Started in Online Investing *(2000)*

One of the greatest disservices you can do a man is to lend him money that he can't pay back.

—Jesse H. Jones (1874–1956)

Net Present Value: in corporate finance, the present value—
that is, the value of cash to be received in the future
expressed in today's dollars—of an investment in excess of
the initial amount invested.

—Nitin Nohria, editorial director,
The Portable MBA Desk Reference *(1998)*

And to preserve their independence, we must not let our
rulers load us with perpetual debt. We must make our elec-
tion between economy and liberty, or profusion and servitude.

—Thomas Jefferson (1743–1826)

Every business (and yours is no exception) has a break-even
point. . . . It is probably the most important number in your
business life. Profit depends on sales volume, selling price,
and costs. A break-even analysis will help you establish
what a change in one of those factors will do to your profits.
To figure out your break-even point, you must separate
your fixed costs (such as rent) from variable costs (such as
cost of goods sold). Break-even point = total fixed costs
minus (1-total variable costs) divided by sales volume.

—Randy Baca Smith, Setting Up Shop: The Do's and
Don'ts of Starting a Small Business *(1982)*

The dynamo of our economic system is self-interest, which
may range from mere petty greed to admirable types of self-
expression.

—Felix Frankfurter (1882–1965)

The ultimate in maximizing profits from a customer list is to be found in the application of the R-F-M formula:

R = Recency of purchase
F = Frequency of purchase
M = Monetary amount

These three criteria are the basis for maximizing profits for all mail order giants.

—*Bob Stone,* Successful Direct Marketing Methods *(1979)*

Everything is sweetened by risk.

—*Alexander Smith,* Of Death and Fear of Dying *(1863)*

Regardless of the compensation system you set up, you must make sure that your company can afford to carry the costs. No optimal ratio between payroll costs and revenue exists, but whatever you decide needs to be a structure that you can handle comfortably. Employees need to feel that their salaries are reasonably well insulated from the ups and downs of your business. Given a choice, most employees might be willing to take home a little less on a yearly basis (within reason) in exchange for the reassurance that they're going to receive their pay regularly throughout the year.

—*Max Messmer,* Human Resources Kit for Dummies *(1999)*

The lack of upside potential differentiates the lenders from the stockholders. Because a lender's return will be at best modest, he or she will work to ensure that any loss incurred will be at best modest. That is, bankers will want to minimize their risk. In lending terms this means that the banker will generally demand collateral. In terms of the business plan, it means the plan must focus on stability and the cash flows necessary to pay the interest in principle required by the loan.

—*William Lasher, Ph.D., CPA,* The Perfect
Business Plan Made Simple *(1994)*

The fundamental idea of modern capitalism is not the right of the individual to possess and enjoy what he has earned, but the thesis that the exercise of this right redounds to the general good.

—*Ralph Barton Perry (1876–1957)*

One-third of the people in the United States promote, while the other two-thirds provide.

—*Will Rogers (1879–1935)*

Financial sense is knowing that certain men will promise to do certain things, and fail.

—*Ed Howe*

You can't see the future through a rearview mirror. I'm convinced that it's the actual memory of the 1929 crash more than any other single factor that continues to keep millions of investors away from stocks and attracts them to bonds, and to money market accounts. Sixty years later, the Crash is still scaring people out of stocks, including people in my generation who weren't even born in 1929.

—*Peter Lynch,* Beating the Street *(1994)*

Money does all things for reward. Some are pious and honest as long as they thrive upon it, but if the devil himself gives better wages, they soon change their party.

—Seneca (ca. 4 B.C.–A.D. 65)

A budget, whether open-ended or constrained by financial resources or profit requirements, necessarily follows a forecast. The budget, too, is a fundamental tool for direct market planning, against which ultimate results are to be evaluated. Budgets can be most effective when they are departmentalized or related to cost centers or profit centers. It is important to recognize that a budget is intended to be a tool of efficient management, not an obstacle or a challenge. . . .

Budgets are of three basic types:

- **New Business Acquisitions:** The cost of promoting, acquiring, and processing new customers. . . .
- **Production:** The fixed and variable costs of providing products and/or services. . . .
- **General/Administration:** The largely fixed costs involved in running an organization.

—Martin Baier, Elements of Direct Marketing *(1983)*

I am not a professional security analyst. I would rather call myself an insecurity analyst.

—George Soros, Soros on Soros *(1995)*

The fact that people will be full of greed, fear, or folly is predictable. The sequence is not predictable.

—Warren Buffet, in Channels *(1986)*

Historically risk takers are people who shatter the illusion of knowledge. They are willing to try something that everyone thinks is outrageous or stupid.

—Daniel Boorstein, historian, in U.S. News & World Report *(1987)*

There are two times in a man's life when he should not speculate: when he can't afford it, and when he can.

—Mark Twain (1835–1910)

Factor future value into every move—make the brand experience exceed the brand perception. As direct interaction with the end user increasingly becomes the prevailing way of doing business, today's brand experience more and more will determine tomorrow's business ranking. What you do to, for, and with the customer that exceeds the brand perception builds brand equity and the future value of the relationship.

—Stan Rapp and Chuck Martin, Max-e-Marketing in the Net Future *(2001)*

When a client refuses to pay you, do you hand the case over to a lawyer? Some entrepreneurs do, but others handle small legal matters on their own by using their attorney as a coach. Lawyers can be very effective in coaching you to file lawsuits in small claims court, drafting employment manuals and completing other routine legal tasks.

—Rieva Lesonsky and the staff at Entrepreneur Magazine, Start Your Own Business *(2000)*

There are at least three very good reasons why a strong relationship with your bank and your banker is to your advantage:

- You and your firm will receive faster and better service from a banker familiar with you and your business;
- Suggestions for keeping your business financially healthy are much more readily given by a bank and a banker informed about your particular business;
- You can avoid costly and harrowing crisis-type borrowing when you plan for your financial needs in a business-like and timely fashion.

> —*Randy Baca Smith,* Setting Up Shop: The Do's and
> Don'ts of Starting a Small Business *(1982)*

People forget that capital markets aren't just supposed to provide capital but also to deny it to companies that can't make efficient use of it.

> —*Professor John Pound of Harvard University, in* Fortune *(1993)*

When the capital development of a country becomes the by-product of a casino, the job is likely to be ill done.

Speculators may do no harm as bubbles on a steady stream of enterprise. But the position is serious when enterprise becomes the bubble on a steady stream of speculation,

> —*John Maynard Keynes (1883–1946)*

Foreign companies . . . want their shares listed in the United States for the same reason that Willie Sutton robbed banks ("that's where the money is").

> —*Janos Surowiecki, in* Slate *(1997)*

Americans have experience derived from the breadth and width of their capital markets. They are people with an extraordinary knowledge of underwriting, financial markets, and above all, capital markets. And they have been able to use this knowledge in a very informative way, which has enabled them to change investment banking from the old-fashioned raising of funds for industry and commerce into the aggressive restructuring of industry.

—Ted Rybczynski, visiting professor,
City University in London,
in The Wall Street Journal *(1996)*

A stockbroker is someone who takes all your money and invests it until it's gone.

—Woody Allen, in The Economist *(1997)*

Real estate is not what moves the economy. The economy is what moves real estate.

—Jane Jacobs, urban economist, in
The Wall Street Journal *(1997)*

The true speculator is one who observes the future and acts before it occurs. Like a surgeon he must be able to search through a mass of complex and contradictory details to the significant facts. Then, like the surgeon, he must operate coldly, clearly, and skillfully on the basis of the facts before him.

—Bernard Baruch, Baruch: My Own Story *(1957)*

Creditors have better memories than debtors.

—*Benjamin Franklin (1706–1790)*

They're scarier than gunslingers.

Quants tend to be bachelors who live in apartments as musty as the room they left in grad school. Many of them drink hard after hours, mostly with fellow workers. They mate, if that's the word, mostly in one-night stands.

—*Article on quantitative analysis,* Time *magazine (1994)*

History cannot be reduced to a set of statistics and probabilities.

—*Alan S. Greenspan, chairman of the*
U.S. Federal Reserve (1992)

It would be hard to find a corporate annual report in my country that does not state "our most important asset is our people"—yet our accounting rules make it literally impossible to reflect this on the balance sheet, and we have just completed a decade in which business after business in the United States has frequently ignored its reality in part because that is not the way we keep score.

—*John Diebold, chairman of the consulting*
firm Diebold Group, Inc. (1991)

Unless it produces action, information is overhead.

—*Thomas Petzinger Jr., in*
The Wall Street Journal *(1997)*

Finance is an art. Not yes or no, right or wrong. It is an art form, an understanding of who should be the companies of the future, and how to structure transactions. It's an art form greatly misunderstood.

—Michael Milken, financier and junk bond popularizer, in Forbes *(1986)*

People call and congratulate us when we buy a company. I say, "Look, don't congratulate us when we buy a company, because any fool can overpay and buy a company, as long as money will last to buy it." I say, "Our job really begins the day we buy the company, and we start working with the management. We start working with where this company is headed."

—Henry R. Kravis, financier, in the Academy of Achievement Web site (1991)

The empirical evidence is clear. In mergers, tender offers, and proxy fights, stockholders of the attacked companies almost always profit.

—Professor Eugene Fama of the University of Chicago, in Time *magazine (1985)*

Synergies are seldom more than constructs for consultants' reports. (Apples and oranges are both fruits from trees, but are grown in totally different environments with differing skills, tools, time frames, and economics. Buying an apple orchard when one already owns an orange grove probably adds rotting apples and eliminates time to care for the oranges.)

—Michael Bloomberg, Bloomberg by Bloomberg *(1996)*

We've found out that if you advertise an interest in buying collies, a lot of people will call hoping to sell you their cocker spaniels. A line from a country song expresses our feeling about new ventures, turnarounds, or auction-like sales: "When the phone don't ring you'll know it's me."

—*Warren Buffett, in* The Berkshire Hathaway Annual Report *(1995)*

He that is of the opinion money will do everything may well be suspected of doing everything for money.

—*Benjamin Franklin (1706–1790)*

Value, Marx argued, was congealed labour. The capitalist's profit—surplus value—therefore could only be created by the labour he employed. The worker, in capitalist society, does not sell the product of his labour, but his capacity to work. What the labourer produces belongs to his master, what he is paid for is his labour and that alone. The capitalist therefore does not pay the worker the value of what he produces; he pays the worker only what is needed to keep the worker alive to produce. The difference between the subsistence wage paid to the worker and the values produced by him is surplus value, on which the capitalist's profit depends.

—The Portable Karl Marx, *edited by Eugene Kamenka (1983)*

I've always believed in cash flow rather than stated profits, because when you state profits, you've got to pay 50 percent to the government. And if you look back at our company over the last 30 years, we've only paid a few million dollars in corporate income tax the entire time. We kept expanding fast enough.... I've been doing that for 30 years and my father did it before me with billboards. He was always trying to keep the depreciation up so he didn't have to pay taxes, and he was able to use his whole cash flow to retire debt.

> —*Ted Turner, founder of Turner Broadcasting,*
> *in* In the Words of Great Business Leaders
> *by Julie M. Fenster (2000)*

One of the chief sources of success in manufacturing is the introduction and strict maintenance of a perfect system of accounting so that responsibility for money or materials can be brought home to every man. Owners who, in the office, would not trust a clerk with five dollars without having a check on him were supplying tons of materials daily to men in the mills without exacting an account of their stewardship by weighing what each returned in the finished form.

> —*Andrew Carnegie, founder of Carnegie Steel,*
> *in* In the Words of Great Business Leaders
> *by Julie M. Fenster (2000)*

THE CUSTOMER

A cornerstone of the marketing concept is customer orientation. Organizations are concerned with creating, caring for, and keeping customers. This implies that customers have value over time way beyond the first sale. . . . Edward C. Bursk, in his article "View Your Customers as Investments" in the *Harvard Business Review,* May–June 1966, observed that "a company's investment in customers can be just as real as its investment in plant and equipment, inventory, working capital, and so forth. And it can be even more valuable in dollars and cents."

—*Martin Baier,* Elements of
Direct Marketing *(1983)*

The most surprising feature of business as it was conducted was the large attention given to finance and the small attention to service. That seemed to me the reversing of the natural process, which is that money should come as the result of work and not before the work.

A dissatisfied customer was regarded not as a man whose trust had been violated, but either as a nuisance or a possible source of more money in fixing up the work which ought to have been done correctly in the first place.

A manufacturer is not through with his customer when a sale is completed. He has only started with his customer.

—Henry Ford, founder of the Ford Motor Company,
My Life and Work *(1922)*

The quest to make GE the most exciting and successful enterprise on earth in this decade will be won on the factory floor, in the field, face to face with customers, with everyone understanding and focused on the essential mission of a corporation: serving customers. . . . At one time, GE executives spent more time on company politics than they did in actual business. People said that GE operated with its face to the CEO and its ass to the customer.

—Jack Welch, CEO of General Electric, in
Jack Welch Speaks *by Janet Lowe (1998)*

I think customer service is really a brilliant system designed to keep customers from ever getting service. My theory is that the most hated group in any company is the customers.

—Dave Barry, in Fortune *(1997)*

What Is a Customer?

- A customer is the most important person ever in this office . . . in person or by mail.
- A customer is not dependent on us. . . . We are dependent on him.
- A customer is not an interruption of our work. . . . He is the purpose of it. We are not doing a favor by serving him. . . . He is doing a favor by giving us the opportunity to do so.
- A customer is not someone to argue or match wits with. Nobody ever won an argument with a customer.

A Raving Fan relationship goes far beyond your company's product. If you don't listen to your customer's thoughts to learn his needs and desires, you will fail to give him what he needs as a product because you simply don't know what that need really is. Further, you reject him as a person. By not listening to him, you're saying his thoughts have no value. . . .

To be consistent you have to have systems. At the core of every great customer service organization is a package of systems and a training program to inculcate those systems into the soul of that company. That's what guarantees consistency.

Delivering your product or service properly time after time without fail is the foundation of Raving Fan Customer Service Systems. This allows you to guarantee delivery— not smiles and "have a nice day."

—*Ken Blanchard and Sheldon Bowles,* Raving Fans *(1993)*

A lot of great computer companies say that marketing services are as important to them as product. But they'll have international product managers, with high status, and no comparable service development manager, who looks after a wide range of services.

—*Laurie Young, marketing consultant, in* The Financial Times *(1997)*

The rise in virtual communities in on-line networks has set in motion the unprecedented shift in power from vendors of goods and services to the customers who buy them. Vendors who understand this transfer of power and choose to capitalize on it by organizing virtual communities will be richly rewarded with both peerless customer loyalty and impressive economic returns. But the race to establish the virtual community belongs to the swift: those who move quickly and aggressively will gain—and likely hold the advantage.

—*John Hagel III and Arthur G. Armstrong,* Net.Gain *(1997)*

If someone thinks they are being mistreated by us, they won't tell five people—they'll tell five thousand.

—*Jeffrey Bezos, founder of Amazon.com,*
in The Wall Street Journal *(1996)*

Our goal as a company [Wal-Mart] is to have customer service that is not just the best but legendary.

—*Sam Walton (1918–1992), CEO of Wal-Mart*

According to Orwell's classic *1984*, the state controlled the screen. In the year 2000 the consumer will control the screen. The computerized shopping screen. The home cocoon will be the site of the future shopping center. All members of the family will be able to shop from one location. Instead of going to the store, the store will come to us, no matter how unusual the product or how frequently needed. On our screens, we'll be able to hear about the latest new products or styles, or order up our old favorites. . . .

Deep at the heart of the vigilante consumer trend is a wish that companies could somehow be more human.

Consumers are willing, even eager, to say "anyone can make a mistake . . . after all, you're only human"—if that, in fact, is the way the company responds. It's not so much "what happened" but whether or not you fix it—quickly, responsibly, and honestly.

—*Faith Popcorn,* The Popcorn Report *(1991)*

Develop a comprehensive customer service training program. . . . Customers hate to wait. Management must practice what it preaches. . . . Develop a customer service mission statement. Communicate it and live it! Develop ways to make your customers more profitable. Hire a good mix of maturity and youth. Occasionally have an employee or family member order from your competitors so you can know how well they serve their customers. Reward customers for referring new clients to you. Educate customers on best ways to use your products and service. Include your customers in your planning. You will be surprised at how much you learn.

—*Byrd Baggett,* Satisfaction Guaranteed *(1994)*

Like the purchasing agent who tells you the only thing they look at is price and so you had best sharpen your pencil, but actually the real priorities are quality and on-time delivery. Like the owner of the computer company who says he wants a case with a unique look, but what he really wants is something as close as he can get to the encasement of the best-selling computer—without being taken to court. That's what I mean by listening to the music as well as to the lyrics.

—*Ken Blanchard and Sheldon Bowles,* Raving Fans *(1993)*

Marketers who don't learn the language of quality improvement, manufacturing, and operations will become as obsolete as buggy whips. The days of functional marketing are gone. We can no longer afford to think of ourselves as market researchers, advertising people, direct marketers, strategists—we have to think of ourselves as customer satisfiers—customer advocates focused on the whole process.

> —*J. Daniel Beckham, "Expect the Unexpected*
> *in Health Care Marketing in the Future"*
> *in* The Academy Bulletin *(1992)*

In our business, the customer service business, the intangibles are far more important than the tangibles. It's not just providing good value—providing a good product at a reasonable price—you need to offer an infusion of spirituality. In other words, if you're in the customer service business, you don't want people just to fly from A to B and say, "Woo, we made it." You want them to get off the plane with the feeling that they were welcome, perhaps entertained. You want it to be a warm event in their lives, so that they will come back.

> —*Herb Kelleher, founder and CEO of Southwest Airlines,*
> *in* Lessons from the Top *by Thomas J. Neff and*
> *James M. Citrin with Paul B. Brown (2001)*

We have found that many tasks that employees performed had nothing to do with meeting customer needs—that is, creating a product high in quality, supplying that product at a fair price, and providing excellent service. Many tasks were done simply to satisfy the internal demands of the company's own organization.

> —*Michael Hammer and James Champly,*
> Reengineering the Corporation:
> A Manifesto for Business *(1994)*

Are your customers demanding more from you, yet looking for ways to pay less? Are you facing a host of new competitors, some of whom you're not even familiar with? Are your customers noticeably more sophisticated in making purchases from you than ever before? If the answer is yes to such questions, you're hardly alone. The new reality is that buyers—both individual customers and business-to-business purchasers alike—can have it all: high quality, excellent service, and a competitive price. Across North America, and spreading rapidly throughout Europe, South America and Japan, a seismic shakeup is altering the relationship between buyers and sellers.

—*Robert B. Tucker,* Win the Value Revolution *(1995)*

Peter Drucker has written that "there is only one valid definition of business purpose: to create a customer." Overcapacity of many global products makes this an especially difficult challenge these days. The balance of power has shifted from producers to consumers, who are high on demands, low on brand loyalties, and skeptical about image manipulations. Consequently CEOs are urging production and marketing behaviors that "live the brand."

—*G. William Dauphinais and Colin Price,*
Straight from the CEO *(1998)*

SALES AND MARKETING

Selling focuses on the needs of the seller; marketing on the needs of the buyer. Selling is preoccupied with the seller's need to convert his product into cash; marketing with the idea of satisfying the needs of the customer by means of the product and the whole cluster of things associated with creating, delivering and finally consuming it.

—Theodore Levitt, "Marketing Myopia"
in The Harvard Business Review *(1960)*

The market demand curve is the horizontal sum of the individual demand curves.

—Jack Hirshleifer and David Hirshleifer,
Price Theory and Applications *(1976)*

Every time I reduce the charge for our car by one dollar, I get a thousand new buyers.

—Henry Ford (1863–1947),
founder of the Ford Motor Company

New and emerging life-styles and value systems of consumers are also major contributors to the growth of direct marketing. Psychographic measurements reflect the changing habits, attitudes, and behavior patterns of a variety of modern life-styles. Direct marketers realize that there is not one single, homogeneous marketplace, but rather that the total market consists of a great many heterogeneous market segments reflecting a variety of contemporary life-styles.

—Martin Baier, Elements of Direct Marketing *(1983)*

How is a fading star transformed into a perpetual money machine? A few hints: premature death. Essential. Aging icons don't sell (see Marlon Brando) but youngish dead ones do (see Marilyn Monroe and James Dean).

Control the brand. "Elvis" and "Elvis Presley" are registered trademarks, which Elvis Presley Enterprises protects with a ferocity Disney would appreciate. . . .

Tackiness sells. . . .

Keep the music coming.

—The Economist *(1997)*

Unfortunately, while the word [positioning] is used by many, very few can accurately come up with the following definition: It's how you differentiate your brand in the minds of your customers and prospects. . . .

You look to the solution to your problem inside the prospect's mind. In other words, since so little of your message is going to get through anyway, you ignore the sending side and concentrate on the receiving end. You concentrate on the perceptions of the prospect. Not the reality of the product.

"In politics," said John Lindsay, "the perception is the reality." So, too, in advertising, in business, in life. . . .

A *People* magazine poll showed that 44 percent of supermarket shoppers didn't know who George Bush was, even though he had been vice president for four years. On the other hand, 93 percent of the consumers recognized Mr. Clean, the genie on the bottle of the Procter & Gamble cleaner of the same name. They recognized Mr. Clean, even though he hadn't been on television in ten years, which shows the power of advertising to register a simple message.

—*Al Ries and Jack Trout,* Positioning *(2001)*

Your company's revenues and profits are also affected by all the discounts and allowances it offers, and so you need to look at these, too. . . .

To achieve real success you have to introduce something that is not only new, but that looks new and different to the market. The product needs a radical distinction, a clear point of difference. Innovations that customers recognize more quickly and easily are those that provide a greater return to the marketer. Researchers who study new product success use the term *intensity* to describe this phenomenon—the more intense the difference between your new product and old products, the more likely the new product is to succeed.

—*Alexander Hiam,* Marketing for Dummies *(1993)*

Note that the market price [in virtual communities] now tracks the supply curve more closely, reflecting the increasing auction-like environments likely to prevail in virtual communities as reverse markets take hold. At that point, when customers want to make a purchase, they notify appropriate vendors and solicit bids. The bidding process tends to create a "mini-market" out of each transaction opportunity, where the clearing price is the winning bid, typically offered by the vendor best able to tailor price and function to the needs of the customer.

—*John Hagel III and Arthur G. Armstrong,* Net.Gain *(1997)*

Two generations ago, Marshall McLuhan proclaimed: "The medium is the message." Marketing's growing dependence on newly arrived TV at that time required a total rethinking of how to build a product brand. Now marketing's new dependence on e-system architecture and customer care software requires a rethink of what is most important in your selling proposition.

—*Stan Rapp and Chuck Martin,*
Max-e-Marketing in the Net Future *(2001)*

Kids can't buy guns, you say? Well, yes and no. Schools can be a huge asset. They collect in one place a large number of minds and bodies that are important to your well-being. What can you do to take advantage of this opportunity? Get to know the principals and coaches at schools in your area. Get them on your side. Impress on them that you'd like to help with the education of children and teachers in the outdoor fields.

—*Grits Gresham, shooting editor of* Sports Afield,
on how to develop the shooting enthusiast market,
in Shoot Business *(1995)*

The sales force needs to see the direct-response-generated lead as an invaluable resource. This doesn't "automatically" happen. Communication networks must be established between marketing and sales departments. Whether the media are mailing pieces, memos, or presentations, the following ideas must be communicated:

- A direct-response-generated lead can be as valuable as a walk-in or a referral and far more valuable than a cold call.
- Direct response is not a hit-or-miss business. There is a precise method, and often a test scheme, behind the generation of the leads the sales force receives.
- For the sake of the system, it's important for a sales person to know that a few unqualified leads received now and then are a necessary evil of the testing process.

—Bob Stone, Successful Direct
Marketing Methods *(1979)*

Here are some "info-bits" that build the knowledge you need to build a relationship. To start, you must develop an information form for your contact management program to store the data: favorite sports team, participant sport, type of car, hobbies, last book read, leisure activities, favorite restaurant, foods, office status symbols, primary goals personal and business, awards won, hometown, birthday, present place of residence, marital status, key views on important issues, colleges attended, belief or faith, number of kids, children's achievements or activities, biggest competition, involvement in organizations.

*—Jeffrey Gitomer, "Collection of Personal
Data Will Help Make the Sale" in*
The San Francisco Times *(2001)*

In the past, if we were trying to sell sushi, we would market it as cold, dead fish.

—Bojan Fazarin of Hewlett-Packard, in Fortune *(1996)*

We don't know how to sell products based on performance. Everything we sell, we sell on image.

—Roberto Guizaeta, former CEO of Coca-Cola,
in The Wall Street Journal *(1997)*

We sell sex. It is never going to go out of style.

—Bob Guccione, publisher of Penthouse *magazine,*
in The Wall Street Journal *(1996)*

People do not need snack foods. Our job as marketers is to entertain and bring happiness to people.

—David J. Guston of the snack-food firm Frito-Lay, in Fortune *(1991)*

"I drive a Volkswagen," says more than who made the automobile the person owns. "I drive a Volkswagen," says something about the owner's way of life. A no-nonsense practical person, self-confident about his or her status in life. A simple, functional piece of transportation equipment.

Utility is the variable whose relative magnitude indicates strength of preference: In finding the most preferred position, the individual maximizes utility. . . . The rational individual will be optimizing—attempting to make the decision that is best in terms of his existing tastes and preferences within the limit of his knowledge and capacity.

—Jack Hirshleifer and David Hirshleifer,
Price Theory and Applications *(1976)*

When we handled the switch from General Electric to GE, we thought we'd get rid of "the meatball"—the GE logo. But it became clear that people all over the world recognized it.

—Hayes Roth of the corporate identity firm Landor
Associates, in Strategy and Business *(1997)*

When baby boomers are 70, they'll eat pizza and listen to the [Rolling] Stones. The popular view that the old are behaving younger is really misplaced. It's rather that the young are becoming older and those habits are sticking with them.

—Bill Whitehead, CEO of Bates North America,
in The Wall Street Journal *(1996)*

It's a hormone-driven business.

—Alan Millstein, retail consultant, in Business Week *(1994)*

If in the past few years we've gained quality, we've done so at a cost: we've lost style. The next wave will be style, and style with a vengeance. It'll be a reaction to the fact that the differences have been leeched out of everything. I call it Hot-Branding. Penetrating the fortress with style, yet keeping quality and function in tact . . .

The Gap is Hot-Branding. When you walk into the Gap, any Gap, you're surrounded by it; it's a total experience.

—Faith Popcorn, The Popcorn Report *(1991)*

Salesmen and saleswomen are taught to sell right now. They are excellent at extracting money in immediate exchange for merchandise. But if the process requires finding the answer to a question or ordering a different model, something happens. Or, to be more accurate, nothing happens.

—Sylvia Rose, marketing trainer and consultant,
in The New York Times *(1996)*

Interpreting and predicting market growth: Over a long period of time, sales (in dollars, units, or as a share of the potential market) will (a) follow a sigmoid growth curve (like a stretched-out, right-leaning S, or sigma in shape), (b) level off to grow at the rate that the customer base grows, and then (c) fall off when a replacement product enters the market. . . . When a market is saturated, you can no longer grow just by finding new customers. Your ambitions are limited by the rate at which customers replace the product and your ability to steal customers from your competitors.

—Alexander Hiam, Marketing for Dummies *(1997)*

The seven steps to developing an offering:
- What is your product?
- Who is the customer of your product?
- What are that person's interests?
- What else does your customer need or desire?
- How can you provide it cost effectively as part of the product offering?
- How can you help your customer understand the full value of this new offering?
- How do you use the service relationship to capture more information?

—Stan Rapp and Chuck Martin,
Max-e-Marketing in the Net Future *(2001)*

Hertz had a huge investment in O. J. Simpson and now all that equity is gone.

—Jed Pearsall, president of Performance Research, in Worth *(1995)*

The value decade is upon us all. If you can't sell a top-quality product at the world's lowest price, you're going to be out of the game. . . . The best way to hold your customers is to constantly figure out how to give more for less.

—Jack Welch, CEO of General Electric

Estimated financial impact of Tiger Woods on the golf industry in millions:
• $4.1 million winnings and appearance money for Woods
• Percent increase in course fees and merchandise sales
• Rise in Tour ticket, concession and souvenir sales
• 10 percent rise in sales of Nike footwear and apparel
• Value of Woods's endorsement deals
• 100 percent increase in value of TV deals for golf
• (total) $653.4 million

—Sports Illustrated (1997)

When Michael [Jordan] was a rookie, I would approach companies and they would say, "David, what on earth are we going to do with a black basketball player?" And I said, "Don't black people use your product?"

—David Falk, sports agent, in The New York Times *(1996)*

You see, there is usually only one thought going through the mind of a bereaved family when they walk through the doors of a funeral home . . . get me out of here. Of course, every funeral director knows this. Which is why the most expensive merchandise is always brought to their attention first—and why, for example, the less expensive caskets are always shown in the ugliest possible colors.

—*Jim St. George, CEO of the coffin maker*
Consumer Casket USA, in Harper's *(1997)*

I tackled my first merchant with the resolve of selling him an order of soap if it took a week. He was located in West Chester, Pennsylvania. He put me off and put me off, but finally broke down; he admitted he would either have to give me an order or kill me. The amount of the order was one dollar and eighty cents. Every man who ever made good with me as a salesman has been a sticker.

—*William J. Wrigley Jr., founder of the Wrigley Company,*
in In the Words of Great Business Leaders
by Julie M. Fenster (2000)

Nordstrom likes to reward good performance in more ways than just sales commissions. In 1968, five years after it went into the department store business and long before it had become a phenomenon, the company established the Pacesetters club as a way of encouraging goal-setting and goal achievement. Pacesetters are sales associates who have set, met and significantly exceeded personal goals. In recognition, they get new business cards that say "Pacesetter" on them. They get treated (with a guest of their choice) to a night on the town. For the next year, their employee discount on Nordstrom merchandise is upped from 20 percent to 33 percent. About one hundred people a year qualify. Just about everybody tries. . . . Every Nordstrom executive started out on the sales floor.

—Ron Zemke with Dick Schaaf, The Service Edge: 101 Companies That Profit from Customer Care *(1989)*

The word "why" is one of the strongest words in the selling language. When some man tells you that he doesn't want the machine you are selling, ask him why, and let him answer before you start telling him why he ought to have it.

—Thomas J. Watson Sr., founder of IBM, in In the Words of Great Business Leaders *by Julie M. Fenster (2000)*

Japanese department stores are clever. Sometimes they don't put escalators next to each other but at a distance, so that customers going up or down walk through sales areas. Foreign customer liaison departments help non-Japanese customers find what they're looking for, and also offer services not sold in the store, like language lessons, moving, and storage. Membership entitles foreigners to discounts at store-sponsored events. Employees at one store wear badges that say "Veteran Golfer" or "Flower Arranger" to identify their hobbies so that customers can relate to them on a more personal level.

—Leonard Koren, 283 Useful Ideas from Japan *(1988)*

ADVERTISING AND PUBLIC RELATIONS

Another reason our messages keep getting lost is the number of products we have invented to take care of our physical and mental needs. . . . In a typical year, the 1500 companies listed on the New York Stock Exchange introduce more than 5,000 "significant" new products. And presumably a lot more than that were insignificant. Not to mention the millions of products and services marketed by America's 5 million other companies.

—*Al Ries and Jack Trout,* Positioning *(2001)*

Few people at the beginning of the nineteenth century needed an adman to tell them what they wanted.

—*John Kenneth Galbraith, in* Crown's Book of Political Quotations, *edited by Michael Jackman (1982)*

If you go out with the idea that you're not going to offend anybody, you probably won't make much of an impression.

—Jamie Barrett of the advertising agency Wieden & Kennedy, in Business Week *(1997)*

Advertising is "the lubricant for the free-enterprise system."

—Leo-Arthur Kelmenson, in The Stein and Day Dictionary of Definitive Quotations, *edited by Michael McKenna (1983)*

Ads are the cave art of the twentieth century.

—Marshall McLuhan, in The Routledge Dictionary of Quotations, *edited by Robert Andrews (1987)*

Advertising is legalized lying.

—H. G. Wells, in Crown's Book of Political Quotations, *edited by Michael Jackman (1982)*

I never tell one client that I cannot attend his sales convention because I have a previous engagement with another client; successful polygamy depends upon pretending to each spouse that she is the only pebble on your beach.

—David Ogilvy, Confessions of an Advertising Man *(1971)*

The most dangerous thing that can happen to us, I think, is to permit a feeling to develop that any client is a problem. I have always taken the attitude that no account is a "problem account" but that all accounts have important problems attached to them—that you can waste more time and burn up more nervous energy by fighting a problem than by taking a positive attitude and solving it. It gives you a nice warm glow when you do.

—Leo Burnett, 100 Leo's

The inventory goes down the elevator every night.

—Fairfax Cone of Foote Cone & Belding, in The Trouble with Advertising *by John O'Toole (1981)*

I'd like to ask each and every one of you how many remarkable people, or people of any kind, you personally have discovered or brought in last year. That is a job I think is too vital for you to delegate. . . . What kind of people should you discover and hire? Well, policemen and tobacco farmers, not MBAs! Hire the kind of people clients don't have and wouldn't dream of hiring. Don't go to clients with a lot of guys who are like theirs, only not so good—you have to remember that clients can afford to pay far more than we can for MBAs.

—David Ogilvy, at an Ogilvy & Mather worldwide meeting (1989)

Great designers seldom make great advertising men, because they get overcome by the beauty of the picture— and forget that merchandise must be sold.

—James Randolph Adams, in The International Dictionary of Thoughts, *edited by John P. Bradley, Leo F. Daniels, and Thomas C. Jones (1969)*

If your advertising goes unnoticed, everything else is academic.
—*William Bernbach,* Bill Bernbach Said ... *(1989)*

Radio, TV, posters, billboards, transit buses, subway signs, T-shirts, flags, calendars, even boat sails are used to communicate marketing messages. ... The point is, the options are many and growing, and your creativity can lead you to media that are fresher and less cluttered than the traditional ones. Anything may go, if you can find a way to make the medium work.
—*Alexander Hiam,* Marketing for Dummies *(1997)*

People are very sophisticated about advertising now. You have to entertain them. You have to present a product honestly and with a tremendous amount of pizzazz and flair, the way it's done in a James Bond movie. But you can't run the same ad over and over again. You have to change your approach constantly to keep getting their attention. ...
—*Mary Wells Lawrence, in* Newsweek *(1966)*

The truth isn't the truth until people believe you, and they can't believe you if they don't know what you're saying, and they can't know what you're saying if they don't listen to you, and they won't listen to you if you're not interesting, and you won't be interesting unless you say things imaginatively, originally, freshly.
—*William Bernbach,* Bill Bernbach Said ... *(1989)*

As advertising becomes the nation's normal idiom, language becomes printed noise.

—*George Will, in* The New York Public Library
Book of Twentieth-Century American Quotations,
edited by Stephen Donadio (1992)

Being myself animated by feelings of affection toward my fellowmen, I am saddened by the modern system of advertising. Whatever evidence it offers enterprise, ingenuity, impudence, and resource in certain individuals, it proves to my mind the wide prevalence of that form of mental degradation, which is called gullibility.

—*Joseph Conrad (1857–1924)*

A man who is hungry need never be told of his need for food. If he is inspired by his appetite, he is immune to the influence of Messrs. Batten, Barton, Durstine & Osborn. The latter are effective with those who are so far removed from physical want that they do not already know what they want.

—*John Kenneth Galbraith, in* Contemporary
Quotations, *edited by James B. Simpson (1964)*

Promise, large promise, is the soul of an advertisement.

—*Samuel Johnson, in* The Columbia Dictionary
of Quotations, *edited by Robert Andrews (1993)*

The headline is the "ticket on the meat." Use it to flag down readers who are prospects for the kind of product you are advertising.

—*David Ogilvy,* Confessions of an Advertising Man *(1971)*

I have discovered the most exciting, the most arduous literary form of all, the most difficult to master, the most pregnant in curious possibilities. I mean the advertisement. . . . It is far easier to write ten passably effective sonnets, good enough to take in the not-too-inquiring critic, than one effective advertisement that will take in a few thousand of the uncritical buying public.

> —*Aldous Huxley, in* The Columbia Dictionary of
> Quotations, *edited by Robert Andrews (1993)*

To Mrs. Mufoosky, the commercials may seem as long as a whore's dream. But to the new advertiser who has spent 100 Gs for his first network commercial—he gets a new understanding of a split second. It's the fastest half minute of his lifetime.

> —*Morris Hite,* Adman: Morris Hite's Methods
> for Winning the Ad Game *(1988)*

Advertising is a valuable economic factor because it is the cheapest way of selling goods, particularly if the goods are worthless.

> —*Sinclair Lewis, in* The New York Public Library
> Book of Twentieth-Century American Quotations,
> *edited by Stephen Donadio (1992)*

Advertising nourishes the consuming power of men. It sets up before a man the goal of a better home, better clothing, better food for himself and his family. It spurs individual exertion and greater production.

> —*Winston Churchill, in* Confessions of an
> Advertising Man *by David Ogilvy (1971)*

There is a great deal of advertising that is much better than the product. When that happens, all that the good advertising will do is put you out of business faster.

—*Jerry Della Famina,* From Those Wonderful
Folks Who Gave You Pearl Harbor *(1971)*

Many a small thing has been made large by the right kind of advertising.

—*Mark Twain, in* The Crown Treasury of Relevant
Quotations, *edited by Edward F. Murphy (1978)*

We grew up founding our dreams on the infinite promise of American advertising. I still believe that one can learn to play the piano by mail and that mud will give you a perfect complexion.

—*Zelda Fitzgerald, in* The Columbia Dictionary
of Quotations, *edited by Robert Andrews (1993)*

The question about those aromatic advertisements that perfume companies are having stitched into magazines these days is this: under the freedoms guaranteed by the First Amendment, is smelling up the place a constitutionally protected form of expression?

—*Calvin Trillin, in* The New York Public Library
Book of Twentieth-Century American Quotations,
edited by Stephen Donadio (1992)

The value of an ad is in inverse ratio to the number of times it has been used.

—*Raymond Rubicam*

I honestly believe that advertising is the most fun you can have with your clothes on.

> —*Jerry Della Famina,* From Those Wonderful
> Folks Who Gave You Pearl Harbor *(1971)*

Historians and archeologists will one day discover that the ads of our time are the richest and most faithful reflections that any society ever made of its entire range of activities.

> —*Marshall McLuhan (1911–1980)*

Advertisements contain the only truths to be relied on in a newspaper.

> —*Thomas Jefferson, in* A New Dictionary of
> Quotations, *edited by H. L. Mencken (1946)*

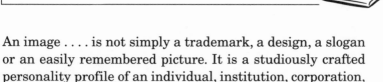

If you tell lies about a product, you will be found out—either by the government, which will prosecute you, or by the consumer, who will punish you by not buying your product a second time.

> —*David Ogilvy,* Confessions of an
> Advertising Man *(1971)*

An image . . . . is not simply a trademark, a design, a slogan or an easily remembered picture. It is a studiously crafted personality profile of an individual, institution, corporation, product or service.

> —*Daniel Boorstin, in* Where the Suckers Moon:
> An Advertising Story *by Randall Rothernberg (1994)*

In day-to-day commerce, television is not so much interested in the business of communications as in the business of delivering audiences to advertisers. People are the merchandise, not the shows. The shows are merely the bait.

—*Les Brown,* Television: The Business Behind the Box *(1971)*

Advertising is a non-moral force, like electricity, which not only illuminates but electrocutes. Its worth to civilization depends upon how it is used.

—*J. Walter Thompson Agency business pitch,*
in Fables of Abundance: A Cultural History of
Advertising in America, *edited by Jackson Lears (1994)*

The vice-president of an advertising agency is a bit of executive fungus that forms on a desk that has been exposed to conference.

—*Fred Allen (1894–1956)*

Christ would be a national advertiser today, I am sure. He was a great advertiser in His own day. He thought of His life as a business.

—*Bruce Barton, in* The New York Public Library
Book of Twentieth-Century American Quotations,
edited by Stephen Donadio (1992)

In American business today, with so many good companies offering bewilderingly similar products, advertising has become perhaps the critical factor in the consumer's decision of which one of those products to buy. The environment is not so much one of innovation as it is one of marketing—which means the adman, more than ever, has become its superstar.

—*Skip Hollandsworth*

At one of the largest advertising agencies in America psychologists on the staff are probing sample humans in an attempt to find out how to identify, and beam messages to, people of high anxiety, body consciousness, hostility, passiveness, and so on.

—*Vance Packard,* The Hidden Persuaders *(1957)*

Let's say you have $1,000,000 tied up in your little company and suddenly your advertising isn't working and sales are going down. And everything depends on it. Your future depends on it, your family's future depends on it, other people's families depend on it. . . . Now, what do you want from me? Fine writing? Or do you want to see the goddamned sales curve stop moving down and start moving up?

—*Rosser Reeves, in* The Art of Writing
Advertising: Conversations with Masters
of the Craft *by Denis Higgins (1990)*

If we define pornography as any message from any communication medium that is intended to arouse sexual excitement, then it is clear that most advertisements are covertly pornographic.

—*Philip Slater, in* The Crown Treasury of Relevant
Quotations, *edited by Edward F. Murphy (1978)*

Advertising has done more to cause the social unrest of the twentieth century than any other single factor.

—Clare Boothe Luce, in Crown's Book of Political Quotations, *edited by Michael Jackman (1982)*

Any ad consciously attended to is comical. Ads are not meant for conscious consumption. They are intended as subliminal pills for the subconscious in order to exercise a hypnotic spell, especially on sociologists.

—Marshall McLuhan, Understanding Media: The Extensions of Man *(1964)*

In the field of marketing . . . the trend toward selling has reached something of a nadir with the unveiling . . . of so-called subliminal projection. That is the technique designed to flash messages past our conscious guard.

—Vance Packard, in The New York Public Library Book of Twentieth-Century Quotations, *edited by Stephen Donadio (1992)*

You know why Madison Avenue advertising has never done well in Harlem? We're the only ones who know what it means to be Brand X.

—Dick Gregory, in The New York Public Library Book of Twentieth-Century Quotations, *edited by Stephen Donadio (1992)*

I know half the money I spend on advertising is wasted, but I can never find out which half.

—John Wannamaker, in Whatever Happened to Madison Avenue? *by Martin Mayer (1991)*

The business that considers itself immune to the necessity for advertising sooner or later finds itself immune to business.

—*Derby Brown, in* The International Dictionary of Thoughts, *edited by John P. Bradley, Leo F. Daniels, and Thomas C. Jones (1969)*

Advertising is a racket, like the movies and brokerage business. You cannot be honest without admitting that its constructive contribution to humanity is exactly minus zero.

—*F. Scott Fitzgerald, in* The Columbia Dictionary of Quotations, *edited by Robert Andrews (1993)*

You must stir it and stump it,
And blow your own trumpet,
Or trust me, you haven't a chance.

—*W. S. Gilbert, in* The New International Dictionary of Quotations, *edited by Margaret Miner and Hugh Rawson (1986)*

If I were starting life over again, I am inclined to think I would go into the advertising business in preference to almost any other. . . . The general raising of the standards of modern civilization among all groups of people during the past half century would have been impossible without the spreading of the knowledge of higher standards by means of advertising.

—*Franklin D. Roosevelt, in* Confessions of an Advertising Man *by David Ogilvy (1978)*

PRODUCTS AND BRANDING

One more thing about the nature of product development today: The boundaries between products and services are fading away. Product companies offer services; service companies offer products; and most companies offer a bundle of products and services.

—Kathleen Allen, Ph.D.,
Entrepreneurship for Dummies *(2001)*

Product life cycle is the process through which a product enters, grows, saturates, and then leaves a market. The product life cycle usually consists of four stages: introduction, growth, maturity, and decline. Each demands a different marketing approach.

—Nitin Nohria, editorial director,
The Portable MBA Desk Reference *(1998)*

History shows that the first brand into the market, on average, gets twice the long-term market share of the no. 2 brand and twice again as much as the no. 3 brand. And the relationships are not easily changed.

You can't create an emotional tie to a bad product because it's not honest.

—Philip Knight, CEO of Nike, in
The Harvard Business Review *(1992)*

The name is the hook that hangs the brand on the product ladder in the prospect's mind. In the positioning era, the single most important marketing decision you can make is what to name the product.... *Esquire* was a great name for the young-man-about-town. When young-men-about-town used to sign their names John J. Smith, Esq. But *Esquire* lost its leadership to *Playboy*. Everybody knows what a playboy is and what he's interested in. Girls, right? But what's an esquire? And what's he interested in?

—Al Ries and Jack Trout, Positioning *(2001)*

Erase the line between product and service—blend services with products to create offerings. No longer is it enough to simply market a product or a service. In the Net Future you will create tightly linked "offerings" without any separation. The fusion of products and services into a preemptive offering will differentiate your selling idea in a commoditized marketplace.

—Stan Rapp and Chuck Martin,
Max-e-Marketing in the Net Future *(2001)*

We'll soon see a dramatic change in "enabling drugs," i.e., anti-stress drugs. Although we know about the future of semi-conductors, we still haven't figured out how to control the biochemistry of the brain. But control it we will.

—Ian A. Martin, chairman and CEO of
Grand Metropolitan Food Sector, in
The Popcorn Report *by Faith Popcorn (1991)*

I'm a brand.

—Martha Stewart, creator of the Martha Stewart
media franchise, in People *(1995)*

I look in my closet, and if I need it, I design it. If it works for me, it works for the customer.

—Donna Karan, in Fortune *(1993)*

The Internet makes it possible to do a complete or partial development of some types of products in cyberspace. Entrepreneurs like Jeff Chappell deliver digital products and services to their customers entirely over the Internet. Chappell discovered the power of the Internet for rapid prototyping and testing. He takes advantage of the free hosting services on the Web to put up a prototype Web site featuring his products and services. When the site garners enough customers to begin to show a profit, he shifts the site over to a full-service ISP and invests more significant marketing dollars into the company at that point. That way, if his product or service isn't working the way he wants it to, he has the option to tweak it or shut down before it costs him a lot of money.

—Kathleen Allen, Ph.D., Entrepreneurship for Dummies *(2001)*

Products may be tangible or intangible. Often they are a combination of both. An automobile is not simply a tangible machine for movement, visibly or measurably differentiated by design, size, color, options, horsepower or miles per gallon. It is also a complex symbol denoting status, taste, rank, achievement, aspiration, and, these days, being "smart"—that is, buying economy rather than display.

—*Theodore Levitt,* The Marketing Imagination *(1983)*

While 3M manufactures and markets nearly seven thousand products and services, loosely organized into about forty-five product lines, most of them are sold to business. That marketing orientation is reflected in a strong business-to-business service culture, whether the product involved is the elastic waistband for disposable diapers or the reflective sheeting used on the faces of traffic control signs. . . . Like many manufacturers, 3M pays attention to maintaining and improving the essential quality of its products. In that context, the official company definition of quality is interesting. "Conformance to customer requirements," is how 3M expresses it. If it doesn't do what the customer wants it to do, in the way and with the reliability that the customer requires, then technical merits notwithstanding, it's the wrong product for the job.

—*Ron Zemke with Dick Schaaf,* The Service Edge: 101 Companies That Profit from Customer Care *(1989)*

How do you deal with unwanted phone calls, including heavy breathers and telephone marketers? Change your number? No. Sony's Telephone Keyboard answering machine offers prerecorded fight-back messages. Access any message by selecting a key when you pick up the phone. Press one key and a threatening male voice yells out, "What the ——— do you want?!" Press another key and the ear of the offending party gets shot with a blast of 100 decibels. The Revenge Telephone (also by Sony) uses an integrated circuit to repeat an obscene message at a caller for as long as he is on the line.

—*Leonard Koren,* 283 Useful Ideas from Japan *(1988)*

The [Wall Street] Journal starts with the premise that it's the availability and the reliability of the news that is important to its customers. That's not a matter of overstating the obvious. In the typical daily newspaper, the amount of news you get is relatively proportional to the amount of advertising sold. *The Journal* uses a different standard: no matter how small each day's version turns out to be on the advertising side, it will always include between 116 and 118 columns of news. . . . That means readers can count on a consistent news product—and the *Journal*'s more than four hundred reporters and editors can do their jobs with that service standard in mind.

—*Ron Zemke with Dick Schaaf,* The Service Edge: 101
Companies That Profit from Customer Care *(1989)*

PRICING

Price is the only element in the marketing mix that produces revenue; the other elements produce costs. Price is also one of the most flexible elements of the marketing mix, in that it can be changed quickly, unlike product features and channel commitments. At the same time, pricing and price competition are the number-one problems facing many marketing executives. Yet many companies do not handle pricing well. The most common mistakes are these: Pricing is too cost oriented; price is not revised often enough to capitalize on market changes; price is set independent of the marketing mix rather than as an intrinsic element of market-positioning strategy, and price is not varied enough for different product items, market segments, and purchase occasions.

—Philip Kotler, Marketing Management *(1994)*

Price is a ratio of quantities: the amount of some good Y that must be given up to obtain a unit of some good X. Thus, one can speak of the price in cigarettes of a hat or the price in labor-hours of a loaf of bread. However, in modern economics, price is normally quoted in terms of money, a medium of exchange. . . . The intersection of demand and supply curves determines the equilibrium values of price and quantities exchanged. . . . If demand increases, equilibrium price and quantity both rise. If supply increases, equilibrium quantity rises but equilibrium price falls.

—*Jack Hirshleifer and David Hirshleifer,*
Price Theory and Applications *(1976)*

Have you established a set of pricing policies?

Have you determined whether to price below, at, or above the market?

Do you set specific markups for each product?

Do you set markups for product categories?

Do you use a one-price policy, rather than bargain with customers?

Do you offer discounts for quantity purchases or to special groups?

Do you set policies so as to cover full costs on every sale?

Have you developed a policy regarding when you will take markdowns and how large they will be?

Do the prices you have established earn planned gross margin?

Do you clearly understand the market forces affecting your pricing methods?

Do you know which products are slow movers and which are fast?

Do you take this into consideration when pricing?

—*A list of pricing questions from* Setting Up Shop:
The Do's and Don'ts of Starting a Small
Business *by Randy Baca Smith (1982)*

Under monopoly there is "too little" market exchange. And in consequence, there will also be "too little" market employment of factors. In effect, monopoly deprives society of some of the mutual benefits of trade.

—Jack Hirshleifer and David Hirshleifer,
Price Theory and Applications *(1976)*

Instead of setting prices based on cost-driven pricing, the Value Innovator does price-driven costing. That is more than a play on words. It means that much more attention is paid to bringing in the product at a price that is in line with what the customer might be able to afford to pay, rather than tacking on a profit margin at the end of a design and build process that considers the ultimate sale price secondarily or hardly at all.

—Robert B. Tucker, Win the Value Revolution *(1995)*

The differences that persist affirm a fixed and ancient dictum of economics—namely, that the world is driven by what happens at the margin or at the appendages, not at the core; that significance attaches not to the common or typical or average condition but rather at the edges of events. Thus, in ordinary competitive analysis, economics affirms that what's important is not the average price but the marginal price, the price at the unstable interface of newly erupting conditions.

—Theodore Levitt, The Marketing Imagination *(1983)*

COMPETITION

The most important way to differentiate your company from your competition, the best way to put distance between you and the crowd, is to do an outstanding job with information. How you gather, manage, and use information will determine whether you win or lose. There are more competitors. There is more information available about them and about the market, which is now global. The winners will be the ones who develop a world-class digital nervous system so that information can easily flow through their companies for maximum and constant learning.

—*Bill Gates,* Business @ the
Speed of Thought *(2001)*

We want to change the competitive landscape by being not just better than our competitors, but by taking quality to a whole new level. We want to make our quality so special, so valuable to our customers, so important to their success, that our products become their only real choice. . . .

The paradox is that these brutally competitive times will be the most exciting, rewarding, and fulfilling for those fortunate enough to be part of boundaryless companies.

—Jack Welch, CEO of General Electric, in
Jack Welch Speaks *by Janet Lowe (1998)*

There are two ways to define competitors who use similar marketing strategies, sell similar products, or have similar skills. Under this definition, you might group Toyota and Nissan as competitors within the car industry. The second, less obvious way to group competitors is by customer—how strongly do they compete for the same customers' dollars? Using this method gives you a wider view of your competition and the challenges they could pose to your new business.

—Rieva Lesonsky and the staff of Entrepreneur
Magazine, Start Your Own Business *(1998)*

Company man or not, we Americans still like to think of ourselves as an independent people, self-reliant, individualistic, and to a degree anarchistic. Compared to Europe, these traits still exist in the American character, but they were developed and reinforced by modes of work that have almost disappeared. The Republic was founded by farmers, craftsmen, proprietors, professionals, and entrepreneurs, and our form of democracy was rooted in the belief that there were enough independent Americans to stand up against demagogues and would-be dictators.

—Michael Maccoby, The Gamesman *(1976)*

From China to Cuba to Vietnam, history teaches the power of a guerilla movement. In business, too, a guerilla has a reservoir of tactical changes that allows the small company to flourish in the land of giants. Size, or course, is relative. The smallest automobile company (American Motors) is considerably larger than the largest shaving company (Gillette). Yet American Motors should fight a guerilla war and Gillette should fight a defensive war. What's more important than your own size is the size of your competition. The key to marketing warfare is to tailor your tactics to your competition, not to your own company.

—Al Ries and Jack Trout, Marketing Warfare *(1986)*

In business, competition is never as healthy as total domination. As a place to invest, I'll take a lousy industry over a great industry anytime. In a lousy industry, one that's growing slowly if at all, the weak drop out and survivors get a bigger share of the market. A company that can capture an ever-increasing share of a stagnant market is a lot better than one that has to struggle to protect a dwindling share of an exciting market.

—Peter Lynch, Beating the Street *(1993)*

A competitive advantage is an edge over other firms in the market. It is something that is used to make your company more attractive and more effective than the competition. Continually coming up with new products that are attractive to customers is a competitive advantage, as is producing extremely reliable products for users whose applications are sensitive to down time.

—William Lasher, Ph.D., CPA, The Perfect
Business Plan Made Simple *(1994)*

Deciding where you want to compete in the virtual community business requires some knowledge of where you can compete. What types of communities are likely to emerge from the many possibilities? What are near- and long-term indicators for profitability and growth? What do we know about a company's assets and skills that can inform us of its chances for future on-line success?

—John Hagel III and Arthur G. Armstrong, Net.Gain *(1997)*

Adam Smith asserted that the invisible hand of self-interest "frequently" leads men to effectually promote the interests of society. Economists in modern times have refined this idea into a more precise theorem that can be worded as follows: "Given a number of ideal conditions, optimizing behavior on the part of individuals and firms under pure competition leads to an efficient . . . social outcome."

—Jack Hirshleifer and David Hirshleifer,
Price Theory and Applications *(1976)*

Gentlemen:

You have undertaken to cheat me. I will not sue you for the law takes too long. I will ruin you.

Sincerely Yours,
C. Vanderbilt

—Cornelius Vanderbilt, to his agents who took over the
Nicaraguan Shipping Line against his will in 1853, in
The Wealthy 100 *by Michael Klepper and Robert Gunther (1996)*

What I can't understand, and what most of the people in my firm still cannot believe, is that none of our American clients, and only a few of the Europeans, has the faintest idea how our system really works. Some of them don't even know what a shosha is and they sure don't know how we function. Of course, that can be a big advantage for us. What I mean is, I'm not surprised if a foreign country doesn't spend time studying the languages or customs of their trading partners. That's something we think is important when you go overseas, but they don't. No problem. But when they miss out on the basics, the kind of things you know they'd never slip up on at home, then I'm surprised. That's bad business.

—A Japanese businessman, in Keiretsu:
Inside the Hidden Japanese Conglomerates
by Kinichi Miyashita and David Russell (1994)

It is to be remembered that oft-times the most difficult competition comes, not from the strong, the intelligent, the conservative competitor, but from the man who is holding on by the eyelids and is ignorant of his costs, and anyway, he's got to "keep running or bust."

*—John D. Rockefeller, founder of Standard Oil,
in* In the Words of Great Business Leaders
by Julie M. Fenster (2000)

There continues to be a tremendous convergence of best practices and skills around the world. The advantages of any superior management know-how and technique are short-lived. Superior awareness, beliefs, and behavior, however, can be a lasting competitive force, hence the spread of such ideas as "transformational change" and "perpetual renewal."

—G. William Dauphinais and Colin Price,
Straight from the CEO *(1998)*

OPERATIONS, PRODUCTIVITY, AND DISTRIBUTION

A typical process of GE generates about 35,000 defects per million, which sounds like a lot, and it is a lot, but it is consistent with the defect levels of most successful companies. That number of defects per million is referred to in the very precise jargon of statistics as about three and one-half sigma (only a handful of companies in the world, several in Japan and Motorola in the United States, have achieved a six sigma level of quality).

—*Jack Welch, CEO of General Electric, in* Jack Welch Speaks *by Janet Lowe (1998)*

Quality is when our customers come back and our products don't.

—*Siemen's quality motto*

Operations Research (OR) has been defined as the systematic, method-oriented study of the basic structure, characteristics, function and relationships of an organization—in order to provide a sound, scientific and quantitative basis for decision-making. Operations researchers are concerned with a variety of problems involving inventory, allocation, queuing, sequencing, routing, replacement, competition and search. . . . The ultimate goal of OR is organization, identifying the most efficient of available alternative courses of action.

—*Martin Baier,* Elements of Direct Marketing *(1983)*

Productivity is a measure of efficiency calculated by dividing output by the total number of hours worked. Output divided by worker hours = productivity. A company can increase its productivity by increasing output, decreasing worker hours, or doing both simultaneously. Other measures of productivity can be devised simply by using a different denominator. Capital productivity, for example, is calculated by dividing output by dollars invested. Materials productivity is determined by dividing output by inventory spending, equipment productivity by dividing output by machine hours, and energy productivity by dividing output by Kilowatt-hours. Each of these is considered a partial-factor measure of productivity that serves to highlight a particular area of management concern.

—*Nitin Noria, editorial director,* The Portable MBA Desk Reference *(1998)*

However, remember productivity is more than just the quantity of work done. It is also the quality. . . . So why do you think people are buying foreign cars? Because American manufacturers did not make enough cars? Or because they did not make the quality car the American public really wanted?

> —*Kenneth Blanchard, Ph.D., and Spencer Johnson, M.D.,*
> The One Minute Manager *(1981)*

Money is a device that reduces the cost of market trading. But it does not, and in the nature of the case cannot, reduce the cost of physical turnovers that are . . . essentially an aspect of production. As regards transportation, for example, geographical dispersion of producers and consumers will dictate shipping costs that would have to be incurred even in a perfectly functioning command economy. Money can do nothing to reduce this shipping cost. And similarly, imperfect synchronization of production and consumption will dictate the presence of commodity inventories at various places along the production turnover–consumption chain. Again, money can't eliminate this category of expense.

> —*Jack Hirshleifer and David Hirshleifer,*
> Price Theory and Applications *(1976)*

The invention of money . . . facilitates the process of exchange and the consequent specialization in production. . . . Under barter conditions firms would therefore tend to be much less specialized, themselves producing a diversity of commodities of interest to their resource suppliers. Money as a medium of exchange promotes specialization in production.

> —*Jack Hirshleifer and David Hirshleifer,*
> Price Theory and Applications *(1976)*

Marketing channels can be viewed as sets of interdependent organizations involved in the process of making a product or service available for use or consumption. . . . Members in the marketing channel perform a number of key functions and participate in the following marketing flows:

- **Information:** The collection and dissemination of marketing research information about potential and current customers, competitors, and other actors and forces in the marketing environment.
- **Promotion:** The development and dissemination of persuasive communications about the offer designed to attract customers.
- **Negotiation:** The attempt to reach final agreement on price and other terms so that transfer of ownership or possession can be effected.
- **Ordering:** The backward communication of intentions to buy the marketing channel members to the manufacturer.
- **Financing:** The acquisition and allocation of funds required to finance inventories at different levels of the marketing channel.
- **Risk Taking:** The assumption of risks connected with carrying out the channel work.
- **Physical Possession:** The successive storage and movement of physical producers from raw materials to the final customers.
- **Payment:** Buyers paying their bills through banks and other financial institutions to the sellers.
- **Title:** The actual transfer of ownership from one organization or person to another.

—Philip Kotler, Marketing Management *(1994)*

Three Observations:

- The computer may be incompetent in itself—that is, unable to do regularly and accurately the work for which it was designed. This kind of incompetence can never be eliminated, because the Peter Principle applies to the plants where computers are designed and manufactured.
- Even when competent in itself, the computer vastly magnifies the results of incompetence in its owners or operators.
- The computer, like a human employee, is subject to the Peter Principle. If it does good work at first, there is a strong tendency to promote it to more responsible tasks, until it reaches its level of incompetence.

—Dr. Laurence J. Peter and Raymond Hull,
The Peter Principle: Why Things Always Go Wrong *(1969)*

The president of an important manufacturing works once boasted to me that their men had chased away the first inspector who had ventured to appear among them, and that they had never been troubled with another since. This was said as a matter of sincere congratulations, but I thought to myself: "This concern will never stand the strain of competition; it is bound to fail when hard times come." The result proved the correctness of my belief. The surest foundation of a manufacturing concern is quality. After that, and a long way after, comes cost.

*—Andrew Carnegie, founder of Carnegie Steel,
in* In the Words of Great Business Leaders
by Julie M. Fenster (2000)

The only way to cut back inventories—particularly in a time of declining business—is to reduce purchases and commitments for materials and supplies. Obvious? Not entirely. Anyway it took us a long time to learn this from experience. In those days the general managers tended to be optimists, as most executives in the selling end of the automobile business were and perhaps still are. They always expected that sales would increase and thereby bring the inventories in line. When the expected sales failed to materialize, a problem arose to which there could be no entirely pleasant solution. Hence we learned to be skeptical of expectation of increased future sales as a solution to a rising inventory problem.

—Alfred P. Sloan Jr., former CEO of General Motors,
in In the Words of Great Business Leaders
by Julie M. Fenster (2000)

I have my flour ground in the old stone mill in Farmington (Connecticut). It was owned by Winchell Smith (a playwright), who ran it for many years. Calvin Coolidge was one of his customers. When Mr. Smith died, he stipulated in his will that the mill should continue under the direction of the same miller and it is from him that I get my flour. It is pure wheat grain, merely ground down with none of its wheat germ removed. This is the element that gives me the greatest satisfaction. I am glad to have succeeded in putting it on a business basis, but I should never sacrifice the health aspects of my bread, no matter how I might be tempted to expand.

—Margaret Rudkin, founder of Pepperidge Farm, in
In the Words of Great Business Leaders
by Julie M. Fenster (2000)

RESEARCH AND DEVELOPMENT

Most marketers underutilize research. These marketers are drivers with no windshield wipers racing down a freeway while wearing work glasses in a rainy night. As long as the road keeps going straight and no competitors switch to their lane, their occasional glimpse of the road is enough to keep them in the race (winning is another matter). But when anything changes, the lack of a clear market view can be fatal.

—Alexander Hiam,
Marketing for Dummies *(1997)*

Far from being objective and trustworthy, statistics are often based on flimsy data and shaped by the prejudices of those who collect them.

—John Micklethwait and Adrian Woolridge,
The Witch Doctors *(1996)*

Time spent in reconnaissance is seldom wasted.

—*Sung Tzu-Wen (1894–1971)*

Although described in the literature in a variety of ways, the basic decision-making process consists of four stages:

- Determine objectives
- Array alternatives
- Deal with uncertainty
- Perform evaluation

It must be emphasized that the proper role of information, as well as calculation, is to enable the direct marketing researcher to make a proper decision. Information and calculation, therefore, are means not ends.

—*Martin Baier,* Elements of Direct Marketing *(1983)*

When doing any type of market research consumer survey, whether it's a focus group, a questionnaire or a phone survey, pay particular attention to customers who complain or give you negative feedback. You don't need to worry about the customers who love your product or service, but the ones who tell you where you're going wrong provide valuable information to help you improve.

—*Rieva Lesonsky and the staff of* Entrepreneur Magazine, Start Your Own Business *(1998)*

The term *population* refers to all the people or things in the group that you are interested in. A sample is a group of items chosen from the population. Because it is expensive, difficult, and sometimes impracticable to survey an entire population, a sample is usually selected for the study. To avoid inaccurate predictions, it is essential that the sample be representative of the population from which it is chosen. Examples of business applications of statistical techniques include the use of samples to estimate the preferences or infer the quality of an entire population, and the use of regression analysis to distinguish the separate effects of several factors. Knowledge of probability concepts helps us to predict the outcome of a process.

—Jeffrey Clark, Ph.D., Business Statistics *(1997)*

Whether you hire a professional market research firm or take on the task yourself, your research should clearly answer the following questions:
- Who will buy the product or service?
- Why will they buy it?
- Where will they buy it—specialty shops, department stores, mail order?
- What do I need to change to make a healthy profit?
- What products or services will mine be competing with?
- Am I positioning my product or service correctly? (In other words, if there's a lot of competition, look for a specialized market niche.)
- What government regulations will my product or service be subject to?

—Rieva Lesonsky and the staff of Entrepreneur
Magazine, Start Your Own Business *(1998)*

Primary research gathers data from people in answer to questions. In general, this type of research gathers data by observing people to see how they behave or by asking them for verbal or written answers to questions. . . . Find a way to observe one of your customers as he or she uses one of your products. I want you to observe, not just watch. Bring along a pad and pencil, and take care to notice the little things.

During the early 1990s, Frito-Lay researchers found that most people preferred a chip that broke under about four pounds of pressure per square inch. And consumers demand consistency. They would complain if chips were just eight one-thousandths of an inch too thick or too thin.

—*Michael McCarthy, in* The Wall Street Journal *(1997)*

Introduction to Probability and Hypothesis Testing:
- Hypothesis testing is a statistical procedure that involves collecting evidence and then making a decision as to whether a particular hypothesis should be accepted or rejected.
- Many common statistical problems are hypothesis-testing problems. The hypothesis being tested is called the null hypothesis, and the hypothesis that says, "The null hypothesis is wrong," is called the alternative hypothesis. In general, it is not possible to prove that the null hypothesis is true or false. After some observations have been collected, however, it is possible to use statistical analysis to determine whether the null hypothesis should be accepted or rejected.

—*Jeffrey Clark, Ph.D.,* Business Statistics *(1997)*

Standard practice in direct mail for many years is to test simultaneously as many as five or six or even ten or twelve different copy appeals, formats, or offers. Giving each package equal exposure over a representative variety of lists is probably the most scientifically precise research method in advertising.

—*Bob Stone,* Successful Direct Marketing Methods *(1979)*

A company must not conclude that it can get a full picture of customer satisfaction and dissatisfaction by simply running a complaint and suggestion system. Studies show that customers are dissatisfied with one out of four purchases and less than 5 percent of dissatisfied customers will complain. . . . Therefore, companies cannot use complaint levels as a measure of customer satisfaction. Responsive companies obtain a direct measure of customer satisfaction by conducting periodic surveys.

—*Philip Kotler,* Marketing Management *(1994)*

Nowadays, Procter & Gamble goes out of its way to talk to, and listen to, its customers. About one million times a year, it phones, visits, or buttonholes customers and potential customers, looking for new market opportunities, ways to improve existing product lines and clues to help it interpret the ever-changing mysteries of consumer behavior. Some of the research is product-specific, assessing everything from performance to the look of labels and packaging. Other inquiries are more wide-ranging, including lifestyle and work style research that tracks the way people handle the mundane details of daily life—fixing meals, cleaning house, and washing clothes, for instance.

—*Ron Zemke with Dick Schaaf,*
The Service Edge: 101 Companies That
Profit from Customer Care *(1989)*

MEETINGS AND NEGOTIATIONS

When you arrange a negotiating session, don't invite one more person than is necessary. (Necessary, in a negotiating session, means that the person has something essential to add to the dialogue that cannot be contributed by someone else.) Compensate for not being able to invite someone by sending that individual a memo. Paper is cheap. Extra voices at a negotiating session can be very expensive. Each person in attendance adds exponentially to the problem of control in communications. The chances of words being uttered when needed rise sharply with each person added to the negotiating team.

—Michael C. Donaldson and Mimi Donaldson,
Negotiating for Dummies *(1996)*

Always be clear about the purpose of a meeting from the outset. If an issue can be resolved without a meeting, cancel the meeting. Consider carefully what makes a successful meeting and what is likely to make an unsuccessful one. Consider what would happen if a regular meeting were not held. Remember the presence of senior managers may inhibit discussions. Hold meetings away from your work space so then you can leave more easily. Familiarize yourself with the different types of formal meeting procedures. Be aware of any legal requirements that are entailed in formal meetings. . . .

Attending a Meeting:
- Work out what you want to say before a meeting begins.
- Brief other participants about problem issues before a meeting.
- Keep your facial expression and tone of voice positive.
- Videotape yourself rehearsing to check that you are being clear.
- Take a deep breath before starting to speak.
- If an idea is your own, take credit for it.
- Do not interrupt other speakers—always let them have their say.
- Use different phrases to make the same point more interesting.
- Identify any areas of agreement when you are negotiating.
- Take personal responsibility for making every meeting a success.
- Encourage those at routine meetings to take turns as chairperson.
- If you reject a motion, try to find at least one area of agreement.
- As a chairperson ensure that all views are heard.

> —*Tim Hindle*, Essential Managers:
> Managing Meetings *(1998)*

The effective man always states at the outset of a meeting the specific purpose and contribution it is to achieve. He makes sure that the meeting addresses itself to this purpose. He does not allow a meeting called to inform to degenerate into a "bull" session in which everyone has bright ideas.

—*Peter Drucker*, The Effective Manager *(1999)*

If you wish information and improvement from the knowledge of others yet at the same time express yourself as firmly fixed in your present opinions, modest sensible men, who do not love disputation, will probably leave you undisturbed in the possession of your error; and by such manner you can seldom hope to recommend yourself in pleasing your hearers or to persuade those whose concurrence you desire.

—*Benjamin Franklin, describing why rigid opinions ultimately fail to persuade, in* Ben Franklin's Twelve Rules of Management *by Blaine McCormick (2000)*

Anger can be an effective negotiating tool, but only as a calculated act, never as a reaction—a photo of Nikita Kruschev's historic shoe-pounding incident at the United Nations revealed that he was still wearing both his shoes. A third "for-pounding-only" shoe. That's calculation.

—*Mark McCormack,* What They Don't Teach You at Harvard Business School *(1984)*

Basically, a threat is an attempt to get something for nothing.

—*H. George McLoszek, industrial management consultant (1992)*

As you sit across the table from the man or woman you'd most like to work for, it is crucial that you relate your skills to what's going on in their head, not merely to what's going on in yours. If I'm dying for lack of a creative artist in my organization, and you walk in and show me you have genuine skills in that area, you are interpreting your skills in terms of my problems. But if I have long since decided I don't need any more help with artwork, and you try to sell me on the idea that I need someone (namely, you), you are falling into the pitfall of interpreting your skills in terms of your problems, not mine.

—*Richard Nelson Bolles,* What Color
Is Your Parachute? *(1972)*

The harder a guy negotiates with us about equity, the better CEO he is likely to be.

—*Henry Kravis, head of the leveraged buyout firm KKR,
in* Merchants of Debt *by George Anders (1992)*

BUSINESS TRENDS

The global battles in virtually every manufacturing industry are now being won or lost on productivity, on speed, on responsiveness to change. The low-skilled, well-paid work of the postwar era has been designed out, or is done in low-wage areas overseas. Companies can no longer hire people who cannot quickly add the type of value required by an ever more demanding and competitive marketplace.

—Jack Welch, CEO of General Electric,
in Jack Welch Speaks *by Janet Lowe (1998)*

Not since John D. Rockefeller sent free lamps to China has the oil industry done anything really outstanding to create demand for its product.

—Theodore Levitt of the Harvard
Business School, "Marketing Myopia"
in The Harvard Business Review *(1975)*

The Americans have need of the telephone, but we do not. We have plenty of messenger boys.

—Sir William Bruce, chief engineer,
Britain's General Post Office, (1876)

People will soon get tired of staring at a plywood box every night.

—Darryl F. Zanuck, movie producer,
on why television won't last (1946)

The problem with all these fossil fuels . . . is that the people increased on earth. We are 6 billion now. When the century started we were a billion and a half. In 30 years, we will be 10 billion, and all of them need energy. . . . Within the next decade or two there will be substantial, inevitable pressure.

—Dr. George Olah, winner of the 1994 Nobel Prize
in chemistry, in The Wall Street Journal *(1998)*

We all have to abide by it or we'll perish. The road to the future is very short. The human being has challenged time. He says: Look at my technology. I have a chain saw and can cut down that black walnut tree in fifteen minutes. It'll take a hundred and fifty years to grow that tree again. The environment will continue as the issue of the nineties. It's going to be the cause of population displacement, disease, questionable food—it's all interrelated. We won't have wars about communism and capitalism—they'll be about land and natural resources.

—Chief Oren Lyons of the Iroquois tribes, in
The Popcorn Report *by Faith Popcorn (1991)*

The trouble in corporate America is that too many people with too much power live in a box (their home), then travel the same road every day to another box (their office). They rarely turn on the TV, because they're swamped with paperwork. And they rarely even scan every page of their newspaper, because they're too consumed with yet a third box, their in box.

—*Faith Popcorn,* The Popcorn Report *(1991)*

If everything we did was absolutely perfect or correct, maybe we'd be given another name and be called God or something. So things didn't work out. We move on to something else.

—*Robert E. Allen, former CEO of AT&T, on cutting 50,000 jobs due to losses incurred during AT&T's adventure in computers, in* The Wall Street Journal *(1996)*

We don't like their sound and guitar music is on the way out.
—*The record company Decca, rejecting the Beatles (1962)*

Virtual communities are not just a stand-alone business opportunity that companies can take or leave as they wish. By shifting power generally from the vendor to the customer, virtual communities will irrevocably alter the way large companies market to customers in their core businesses. These changes will demand new ways of thinking about and approaching the marketing and sales functions.
—*John Hagel III and Arthur G. Armstrong,* Net.Gain *(1997)*

Open telecom markets may ultimately save consumers money, but in the short term, the main beneficiaries are some very busy telecom lawyers.

—Amy Barrett, in Business Week *(1996)*

The top 500 companies in the United States will spend close to $100 billion on information technology in 1996. This is equivalent to approximately $6,000 per employee on average.

—Dr. Howard Rubin, CEO of Rubin Systems (1996)

The dichotomy of American retailing continues. The upper-income stores will continue to do well, as will the lower-end stores because they offer value. And the guys in the middle seem to have the problems.

*—Jeffry Ferner of the investment bank Lehman Brothers,
in* The New York Times *(1997)*

The sicker you make a patient look, the more money you get. Most doctors don't really understand how that system works. Physicians are angry about the loss of control. I look at big profits being raked off by for-profit HMOs instead of going to physicians for working hard. We've sort of gone from a profession to a service industry. . . . The individual companies think it's all widgets and algorithms. If you're a bad widget, we'll get rid of you; if you're a good widget, it doesn't matter which widget you are.

—Dr. Debra Shapiro, in The New York Times Magazine *(1997)*

It's a painful shakeout. Steel has gone through it, farmers, and computers. We doctors have always occupied a very favored position. Now it's our turn.

—Dr. Richard Egdahl, director of Boston University Medical Center, in U.S. News & World Report *(1987)*

Until recently, the closest thing to a risky decision in America's defense industry was selecting a Washington restaurant in which to entertain a Pentagon contact.

—The Economist *(1992)*

I grew up in the Great Depression. I know that banks failed not because I read about them in newspapers but because my mother and her friends lined up in panic at the United States Bank at 170th Street off the Grand Concourse in the Bronx to find her savings gone. I saw my friends' fathers— heads of households who drove taxis or sewed or sold cloth or fur—drift home and weep from fear and shame as they lost their jobs, their savings, and their dreams. In those days, there was no unemployment insurance, no Social Security, and no Welfare—when you lost everything, you had nothing left.

—Lester Wunderman, a direct marketing pioneer and chairman of Wunderman Cato Johnson (1996)

Over the past twenty-five years economic forecasters have missed four of the past five recessions.

—Business Week *(1996)*

GOVERNMENT AND BUSINESS

One of the most dramatic failures of government has been the case of regulatory agencies. Even the strongest critics of the market and warmest supporters of government will agree that these organizations have become the servants of those they were supposed to protect government from.

—Milton Friedman, Nobel Prize–winning economist, in Playboy *(1973)*

Eventually more business people will get involved in making the political process work again. Hopefully, in the future, it will be safe to run for office. The media will stop destroying reputations, and focus instead on what a person's contributions will be.

—Richard Gillman, chairman of the board of Bally's Park Place Casino Hotel, in The Popcorn Report *by Faith Popcorn (1991)*

I sincerely believe that banking establishments are more dangerous than standing armies.

—*Thomas Jefferson (1815)*

How does a government measure capital formation, when new capital is intellectual? How does it measure the productivity of knowledge workers whose product cannot be counted on your fingers? If it cannot do that, how can it track productivity growth? How does it track or control the money supply when the financial markets create new financial instruments faster than the regulators can keep up with them? And if it cannot do these things with the relative precision of simpler times, what becomes of the great mission of modern governments controlling and manipulating the national economy?

—*Walter B. Wriston, former CEO of Citicorp (1993)*

Without even considering the state's threat to individual liberty, there are at least three practical reasons why its demands may in fact damage corporations. First, because of national security, new technology for the state cannot be sold to other potential buyers. . . . Second, corporations find that dependence on the state encourages bad business practices. Building whatever is technically possible is poor business for a company competing in a tight international market. Third, dependence on the state is risky, since a change in national policy can suddenly upset all corporate planning. . . . Demands of the state can cramp corporate planning processes and endanger the competitive position of highly technological companies. Corporations most dependent on the state have often ended up ill equipped to compete in a world market.

—*Michael Maccoby,* The Gamesman *(1976)*

Three things must exist for electronic commerce to prosper. Ease, ubiquity and trust. Technology can take care of the first two. But how can consumers be sure that their transactions are secure and private? The question we're grappling with is whether government has a role in creating that trust.

—Christine Varney, member of the Federal Trade Commission, in The New York Times *(1997)*

This is called capitalism. We create a product called Windows. Who directs what's in Windows? It's the customers who buy Windows.

—Bill Gates, CEO of Microsoft, reacting to an antitrust action against his company, in The Wall Street Journal *(1997)*

The difference in prices of distilled spirits between states are mainly due to differences in liquor taxation. (In some states liquor is a state monopoly, in which case a high monopoly price is substantially equivalent to a high tax.) Very small sensitivity of quantity purchased to price (inelastic demand) is convenient if the purpose of the tax is simply to generate tax revenues. But if the purpose is to discourage consumption, it appears that liquor taxation is not very effective.

—Jack Hirshleifer and David Hirshleifer, Price Theory and Applications *(1976)*

Why does a slight tax increase cost you two hundred dollars and a substantial tax cut save you thirty cents?

—Peg Bracken, humorist

As an investor in small companies, I don't care how rich Microsoft is. I care about what my opportunities are. If I had the sense that Microsoft was genuinely holding back the market then I'd care. But I don't think they are.

—*Esther Dyson, president of the high-tech
investment company Edventure Holdings,
in* The Wall Street Journal *(1997)*

Unlike other industries, our pace of change is so fast that I don't think it's right to expect the same type of concentration as in the auto industry.

—*Michael Dell, CEO of Dell Computer,
in* The Wall Street Journal *(1997)*

The best estimate of the regulating burden . . . puts the cost of complying with federal rules at $668 billion in 1995 compared with $1.5 trillion in federal spending. In 1995 federal regulation cost the average American household $7,000 (more than the average income-tax bill, which was $6,000 per household).

—*Thomas Hopkins of the Rochester Institute of
Technology, in* The Economist *(1996)*

Chrysler's 1991 return . . . was a stack of paper six feet high, prepared by fifty-five accountants who worked on nothing else that year. The company is perpetually audited by at least nine IRS agents. Chrysler's chief tax counsel estimates that it will be ten years before all current matters in dispute between Chrysler and the IRS are settled.

—*American Heritage (1996)*

There would be no income tax. I know of no statesman or authority who does not denounce an income tax as the most objectionable of all taxes. Mr. Gladstone once appealed to the country upon this subject alone, denouncing it as tending to make a nation of liars. While it is in theory a just tax, in practice it is the source of such demoralization as renders it perhaps the most pernicious form of taxation which has ever been conceived since human society has settled into peaceful government.

> —*Andrew Carnegie, founder of Carnegie Steel, in* In the Words of Great Business Leaders *by Julie M. Fenster (2000)*

It is noteworthy that the United States is the one important nation in which broadcasting has not been made a government monopoly. Here, radio has been from the beginning not an instrument made by the government, but rather an instrument for the making of government.

> —*William S. Paley, founder of CBS, in* In the Words of Great Business Leaders *by Julie M. Fenster (2000)*

Experiences in the United States during the past twenty years have reinforced support for economic deregulation both here and abroad. Nevertheless, government still has an active role to play in deregulated markets. Indeed, government must vigorously enforce anti-trust laws, encourage the provision of accurate and easily understood prepurchase information, aggressively administer consumer protection provisions, and extend protection to potentially vulnerable consumer groups if society is to enjoy the maximum benefit of economic deregulation.

> —*Cathleen D. Zick, "Economic Deregulation" in* Encyclopedia of Consumer Movement, *edited by Stephen Brobeck (1997)*

THE GLOBAL ECONOMY

The new model is global in scale, an interdependent network. So the new leaders face new tests such as how to lead in this idea-intensive, interdependent-network environment. It requires a wholly different set of skills, based on ideas, people skills, and values.

—John Scully, former CEO of Apple Computer, in "Leaders on Leadership" by Warren Benn in The Harvard Business Review *(1991)*

After five years in the States, I've changed my mind about prospects for the future. The tremendous asset in this country is the people. Americans, by and large, have a positive attitude about the future, which is very different from Europeans, who are much more cynical because of their history. And they're proud of being cynical.

—Patrick Chael, chairman of Elida Gibbs-Faberge, in The Popcorn Report *by Faith Popcorn (1991)*

The challenge facing the United States is how do we justify our high wages. The answer is to remain innovative, to use American creativity to continue inventing things of greater value, specialty steels instead of basic steels, the next drugs, the new semiconductor chips, the financial services never thought of by anybody before.

—*Professor Michael Porter of the Harvard Business School, in* The Wall Street Journal *(1997)*

"Big Ideas" are going to push America ahead in business and help us to outdistance the competition from abroad. Corporations and individuals will need to agree on priorities for our society and then make them happen. There may indeed be an international economy on the verge of burgeoning, and Americans will need to compete for our fair share of the international dollar. Our inventiveness and foresightedness are going to be called on as never before.

—*Sander A. Pflaum, president and CEO of Robert A. Becker, Inc., in* The Popcorn Report *by Faith Popcorn (1991)*

How can you be the world's leading power when you're the world's leading borrower? It's the lenders who have the leverage.

—*Peter G. Peterson, former chairman of the Blackstone Group*

We were doing very well as long as the game was played on our court with our rules, our balls, and our level of proficiency. But here comes somebody who says, "I play the same game, with the same balls, but I have this new racquet and this new technique. And I've been practicing a lot, and I'm a perfectionist. And whereas these guys practice three hours a day and then go to the clubhouse for a drink, we practice twelve hours a day, seven days a week. And we learn everything there is to know about the game."

—Professor Martin Starr of the Columbia University Business School, in The Chip War *by Fred Washofsky (1989)*

General Motors wondered why its Chevy Nova, which was selling spectacularly in the United States, had dismal sales in South America. After research revealed that "no va" means "it won't go" in Spanish, it renamed the car Caribe.

—Richard Bucher, Diversity Consciousness *(2000)*

Companies used to buy [kidnapping] coverage only for their most senior people. But as companies are working much more in the third world, places like Russia and Latin America, virtually all their employees, anywhere in the world, are being covered. Family members and even guests of employees are covered.

—Mack F. Rice Jr. of the insurance brokers Marsh & McLennon, in The New York Times *(1997)*

A Mercedes has enormous cachet in Britain, but in Germany it is a taxi.

—Donald Gunn, director of creative resources at the Leo Burnett ad agency, in The New Yorker *(1997)*

Global products are often tacky things built to suit the lowest common denominator.

—The Economist (1996)

McDonald's serves wine and salads with its burgers in France. For the Indian market, where beef products are taboo, it created a mutton burger: the Maharaja Mac.

—John Williams, in The Financial Times *(1997)*

If you want to take on the world, the world better like your product.

—John Wakely of Shearson Lehman, London, in
The Wall Street Journal *(1996)*

The events we see rushing toward us make the rough, tumultuous eighties look like a decade at the beach. Ahead of us are Darwinian shakeouts in every major marketplace, with no consolation prizes for the losing companies and nations.

—Jack Welch, CEO of General Electric, in
"The Return of Karl Marx" in The New Yorker *(1997)*

If you want to see where the Russian Money is, go to New York, London, or Paris.

—A spokesman for the Central Bank of Cyprus,
in The Wall Street Journal *(1996)*

Communism may have been defeated, but the communists often have not been.

—Margaret Thatcher, former prime minister
of England, in Fortune *(1993)*

Every country that has caught up has done it by copying.

—Professor Lester C. Thurow, Sloan School of Management,
MIT, in The Harvard Business Review *(1997)*

Corporations are frequently more powerful than countries. Indeed, these days, so are some individuals. We live in a capitalistic age. It is not a negative concept that someone's wealth is greater than the GDP of some countries.

Are we above governments? No. We answer to governments. We obey laws in every country in which we operate. However, we do change relations between countries. We function as a lubricant for worldwide economic integration.

—*Marc Faber, Hong Kong investment expert,*
Asia Inc. Online (1995)

People in the United States get very excited that RCA developed the transistor but the commercialization really occurred in Japan. But if we're not smart enough to commercialize it, that's not their problem. That's our problem. You win by moving quicker than your competition, not by trying to build walls.

—*Philip Condit, CEO of Boeing,*
in The Financial Times *(1997)*

When I was first interviewed for a job at Honda, one executive asked me what my future goals were. I responded, "I want to design racing engines. There's an idea I have about valve train design and I want to test it out. If Honda won't let me do that, I don't want to work here." The executive looked stunned at my last comment, but he was not impressed with my goal. He said, "Young people these days do not seem to have very big dreams. I was expecting you to say that your goal was to become president of the company."

—*Shoichiro Irammajiri, president of Honda*
of America manufacturing (1987)

It's a war here, and we love a war. We're not defenders, we're predators.

—David Hancock, president of Hitachi's U.S. personal computer unit, in The Wall Street Journal *(1996)*

On presenting a suitcase full of used $100 bills to your favorite government official, it is always best to say: "Here you are, old man, you left this at my office the other day. Thought I'd take the opportunity to return it."

—Charles Dubow, in Forbes *(1997)*

If an American wants an answer he'll pick up the phone. A European will write a memo. The phone call will seem overly aggressive and pushy to the European manager, but the American needs to convey a greater sense of urgency because competition in the United States is so tough.

—Kai Lindholst of the international consulting firm Egon Zehnda, in Time *(1989)*

American schools teach international business as a subject. At Insead (a business school in France), it's integrated throughout the curriculum. At Insead it's the reason for being. The fact that the United States is no longer the sole driving engine of the world economy has created more need for international focus.

—Daniel Mazyka, an American who teaches at the French business school Insead, in The New York Times *(1991)*

New behaviors in all facets of management are demanded by the uncoupling of the corporation from the nation-state.

Rapid free flows of technology, capital, and employment contribute to this "global village" effect. Many CEOs realize that they have to begin to break out of their old Euro- and U.S.-centered values and approaches.

—*G. William Dauphinais and Colin Price,*
Straight from the CEO *(1998)*

These K'retsu, as he called them, were industrial juggernauts that virtually controlled Japanese business and were already preparing to bulldoze their way across the globe in search of new conquests. Although they kept up a fierce level of competition at home, when foreign smoke signals were visible on the horizon, they would forget about their own squabbles long enough to pull the wagons in a circle and fight off the invader.

—*Kenichi Miyashita and David Russell,* Keiretsu: Inside
the Hidden Japanese Conglomerates *(1994)*

The Alcatel Group was originally French. However, since France represents 22 percent of our market share worldwide, it's now absolutely key for us to have a mixture of nationalities on our team, as well as in each country. Our working language is English, and among the five hundred managers and directors in the group, fewer than 30 percent are French. The executive committee, which is responsible for Alcatel Telecom, consists of six members, including a Belgian, an American, three Frenchmen, and one Frenchwoman. . . .

My entire professional career has taken place in an international environment. I don't differentiate between nationalities, and I don't believe there are basic cultural differences. The notion that individuals in a company will behave according to the stereotypes of their home countries' culture is an erroneous cliché. What is important in our group is the culture of Alcatel.

—Serge Tchuruk, CEO of Alcatel Alsthom, "Driving Fundamental Change at Alcatel: A New Prism on Customer Focus" in Straight from the CEO, *edited by G. William Dauphinais and Colin Price (1998)*

CEOs are increasingly acting as global brand managers in successful knowledge-based companies, while product sales and manufacturing are in consistent flux around the world. Whether the company is selling children's wear or semiconductors, it's up to the CEO to maintain and expand a consistent and coherent image for his or her company. This is as true for OshKosh B'Gosh as it is for Nike or The Gap, which are marketers more than anything else, having shifted production to lower-cost offshore markets.

—Douglas Hyde, CEO of OshKosh B'Gosh, Inc., "New Products That Remain True to Core Values" in Straight from the CEO, *edited by G. William Dauphinais and Colin Price (1998)*

All business organizations need to be increasingly efficient because of the growth of competition; an international company may face this particular pressure on many fronts. . . . Any company wishing to enter foreign markets must choose between fundamentally different alternatives before it begins to form its plans. The decision lies between whether to extend the duties of the domestic company to overseas operations, or to create a specialist international company, division or department.

—Richard L. T. Bickers, Marketing in Europe *(1971)*

It is no longer a compelling point of pride to declare: "Our company has offices—or factories—in x countries worldwide." All the best competitors meet that mark, and so much more is expected. Genuine points of pride have to do with global coordination coupled with well-accepted local identities—the achievement of a global brand with satisfied and enthusiastic local buyers. This is hard enough for companies that manufacture and distribute products. It is harder still for companies that rely primarily on intellectual capital to produce valued solutions for clients.

It is also clear that the corporate provider of goods and services must bring to bear its full competitive muscle everywhere it operates in order to generate scale. A dominant position in just a handful of world markets is unlikely to last in today's environment.

—James J. Shiro, CEO of Price Waterhouse, "The New Phase of Globalization" in Straight from the CEO, *edited by G. William Dauphinais and Colin Price (1998)*

The old multinational corporations were quasi-colonial institutions that used the less-developed world as a dumping ground for secondhand technology, and often for second-rate executives. They can't profitably do that today because of the democratization of technology, capital, and management know-how. The new factories going up in Asia and Latin America have the benefit of low wages and state-of-the-art technology. Five years ago a prediction that Bangladore, India, would become a world-class software center would have been absurd. Not anymore. In the future, we can expect centers of excellence in other technologies to crop up in many formerly unlikely places.

—G. William Dauphinais and Colin Price,
Straight from the CEO *(1998)*

ENTREPRENEURSHIP

According to many experts, the final element that determines whether you are ready to become an entrepreneur is if you are able to raise significant amounts of money from investors. If you can make other people believe in your dream and share your goals so that they are willing to invest hard-earned cash in your venture, chances are you have what it takes.

—*Rieva Lesonsky and the staff of* Entrepreneur Magazine, Start Your Own Business *(2000)*

Business demands innovation. There is a constant need to feel around the fringes, to test the edges, but business schools, out of necessity, are condemned to teach the past. This not only perpetuates conventional thinking, it stifles innovation. I once heard someone say that if Thomas Edison had gone to business school we would all be reading by larger candles.

—*Mark McCormack,* What They Don't Teach You at Harvard Business School *(1984)*

There is a basic financing fact that should be understood at the outset by anyone interested in starting their own business. Most of the money behind small business start-ups comes from the entrepreneurs themselves and from family and friends. . . . More to the point, it's rarely realistic to assume that you can start your own business without any of your own money.

—*William Lasher, Ph.D., CPA,* The Perfect
Business Plan Made Simple *(1994)*

Just take a look at some of the fallacious reasons people give for wanting to own and operate their own businesses:
- I'm tired of working for someone else.
- I'll be able to do exactly what I please!
- I don't like taking orders.
- I'll be able to take time off whenever I want to play golf, gin rummy, etc., go skiing, chase women/men, go on vacation.

When you're the "here" at which the buck stops, a lot of other things stop, too. Mainly the fun stuff.

—*Randy Baca Smith,* Setting Up Shop: The Do's
and Don'ts of Starting a Small Business *(1982)*

Your family has to understand the work hours and craziness associated with a start-up.

—*Mark Biestman, who left Oracle to help start up
Netscape, in* The Wall Street Journal *(1996)*

Ideas are a commodity. Execution of them is not.

—*Michael Dell, CEO of Dell Computer,
in* Fortune *(1993)*

Most of the guys who failed are the ones who stopped listening and got carried away with their own ego. All of a sudden they became folk heroes and started to believe their own public relations.

—William Hambrecht, cofounder of the investment bank Hambrecht & Quist, in Time *magazine (1984)*

Entrepreneurs are men who build big organizations and have intense unresolved rivalries with their fathers.

—Harry Levinson, clinical psychologist and president of the consulting firm Levinson Institute, in U.S. News & World Report *(1987)*

I think it is unfortunate that to some degree the word "entrepreneur" has taken on the connotation of a gambler. I don't see it that way at all. Many times action is not the most risky path. The most risky path is inaction.

—Fred Smith, founder of FedEx, in The Entrepreneurs— an American Adventure *by Robert Sobel and David B. Sicilia (1986)*

Experts agree, the best place to look for ideas is to start with what you know. . . . Don't forget those old standbys. New communities always need dry-cleaning shops, ice cream stores, cleaning services (think carpet cleaners, janitorial services), etc. Remember the new creed the American consumer lives by: value and convenience.

—Rieva Lesonsky and the staff of Entrepreneurial Magazine, Start Your Own Business *(2000)*

When I first started in the electronics field forty years ago, a few hundred dollars' worth of instrumentation was all you needed. Today, you can't work at the frontiers of technology and electronics without equipment costing millions of dollars.

—David Packard, cofounder of the computer company
Hewlett-Packard, in U.S. News & World Report *(1987)*

The entertainment industry is now the driving force for new technology, as defense used to be. Making a dinosaur for *Jurassic Park* is exactly the same as designing a car.

—Edward R. McCracken, CEO of Silicon Graphics,
in Business Week *(1994)*

I've worked with hundreds of entrepreneurs and I've never met one who said, "I want to get rich" who did. The successful ones say, "I want to find a way to do animation faster," or "I'm really interested in adhesion."

—Professor John Goodman of the University
of Southern California, in Fortune *(1995)*

After Apple hit, Steve Jobs [founder of Apple] began wearing Armani and having lunch with Jerry Brown. He even got an apartment on Central Park. I don't finance guys who have lunch with Jerry Brown and have apartments 3,000 miles away. I want a guy who doesn't even know who the president is. Someone driven to a single agenda, to 15-hour days and six-day weeks.

—Don Valentine, Silicon Valley venture
capitalist, in Worth *(1996)*

To me one of the most exciting things in the world is being poor. Survival is such an exciting challenge.

—Thomas Monaghan, founder of Dominos Pizza

I never met a rich pessimist.

—Allen Breed, chairman and CEO of
Breed Technologies, Inc. (1995)

In fact, it was at a pay phone across the street from the People's computer office here [the People's Computer Company in Menlo Park, California] where a government informer caught him in the act of telephone fraud.

This time Mr. Draper went to prison, spending October 1976 to February 1977 at the federal prison in Lompoc, California. For the final portion of his sentence he was in a work-release program back in the San Francisco Bay Area, where he began developing his EasyWriter program.

During the day, he recalled, he would write the code. Then, at night, after returning to jail, he would study the paper list of programming commands, looking for errors. "It was an ideal situation," he said, "it forced me to get off the computer and think and debug my program."

—John Markoff, "The Odyssey of a Hacker: From an
Outlaw to a Consultant" in The New York Times *(2001)*

If you felt unfulfilled at your job for a long time, chances are you'll harbor resentment toward your past employer after you start your own business. But if you leave a job because you are angry, be sure not to transfer your anger to your new business, or failure is almost certain. Once you start

your own business, you must leave behind any bad feeling
about your former job or boss.

> —*Rieva Lesonsky and the staff of* Entrepreneur
> Magazine, Start Your Own Business *(2000)*

As part of the buyout, Cohen managed to wrest an agreement from Unilever to set up a $5 million fund to encourage
small-business development for the poor and to leave him
on the board of Ben and Jerry's, in charge of socially responsible practices. He would consult with the larger company
on its social mission and most importantly Ben and Jerry's
headquarters would stay in Vermont—where it supports
small dairy farmers and is a keystone of the local economy.

> —*Claudia Dreifus on Ben and Jerry's cofounder*
> *Ben Cohen's reaction to the Unilever takeover of his company,*
> *"The Emperors of Ice Cream" in* My Generation *(2000)*

More than 14 million people are involved in home-based
business. Why is starting a business from home so popular?
I find several reasons:
• Because of technology, in particular the Internet, people
  can run their business from anywhere just by going on-line.
• Because more resources are available to entrepreneurial
  businesses than ever.
• Because tax laws have grown friendlier to home-based
  businesses.

> —*Kathleen Allen, Ph.D.,* Entrepreneurship for Dummies *(2001)*

The searcher for the new conforms to the well-established
idea of what people should do for a living. He gropes.
Finding the new new thing is as much a matter of timing as

of technical or financial aptitude, though both of those qualities help. . . . The person who makes his living searching for the new new thing is not like most people, however. He does not seriously want to sink back into any chair. He needs to keep on groping. He chooses to live with that sweet tingling discomfort of not quite knowing what it is he wants to say. It's one of the little ironies of economic progress that, while it often results in greater levels of comfort, it depends on people who prefer not to get too comfortable.

—Michael Lewis, The New New Thing *(2000)*

Quite frankly, the bigger question is how you retain an appropriate level of entrepreneurialism inside the company. Because to not be an entrepreneur even at the Jack Welch level, is to begin the process of decline and decay. You always have to be an entrepreneur, otherwise you will fall behind. The question is how you manage to be entrepreneurial in a progressively larger enterprise, and still provide the appropriate administrative oversight and direction.

—Fred Smith, founder and CEO of FedEx,
in Lessons from the Top *by Thomas J. Neff and*
James M. Citrin with Paul B. Brown (2001)

TECHNOLOGY AND THE WEB

In the frenzy that followed, a lot of old rules of capitalism were suspended. For instance, it had long been a rule of thumb with the Silicon Valley venture capitalists that they didn't peddle a new technology company to the investing public until it had at least four consecutive profitable quarters. Netscape had nothing to show but massive losses. But its fabulous stock market success created a precedent. No longer did you need to show profits; you needed to show rapid growth. Having a past actually counted against a company, for a past was a record, and a record was a sign of a company's limitations.

—*Michael Lewis,*
The New New Thing *(2000)*

Trying to assess the true importance and function of the Net now is like asking the Wright brothers at Kitty Hawk if they were aware of the potential of American Airline's Advantage miles.

—Brian Terren, head of Imagineers, Disney's creative think tank, in The New Yorker *(1997)*

It's important to step back from an industry that is full of people announcing new widgets every day—faster widgets, more widgets—what I'm learning from customers is that there is an excess of technology out there. The real pressure is, how do I use this stuff to achieve something important for my business?

—Louis V. Gerstner Jr., CEO of IBM, in Fortune *(1997)*

For those who will be receiving a PC from Santa, remember: a computer is a gift that keeps on taking.

—Peter H. Lewis, in The New York Times *(1996)*

One of the most startling turnarounds in the Net economy is the way in which information sharing with traditional competitors can now provide a business advantage. In a world that is constantly evolving, the more people you have on your side—even if those connections are temporary and subject to change—the better chance you have of finding out what you need to know to survive. Alliances have become the new currency of commerce and companies will soon be outpaced by the competitors working together to build a more productive environment.

—Stan Rapp and Chick Martin, Max-e-Marketing in the Net Future *(2001)*

People usually compare the computer to the head of a human being. I would say that the hardware is the bone of the head. The semiconductor is the brain within the head. The software is the wisdom. And the data is the knowledge.

—Mashayoshi Son, founder and CEO of Softbank Corp.,
in The Harvard Business Review *(1992)*

In our experience, the number one thing that keeps the senior management of large companies from launching a virtual community is discomfort with technology choices required to be successful. (The entrepreneurs we've run across tend to be a bit more comfortable with this issue.) At one level this discomfort is understandable. It's all too easy, on venturing into cyberspace, to become seduced or overwhelmed by the magnitude of technological options available. Yet it's quite possible to overcome this discomfort by staying focused on member needs and by adhering closely to the principles of speed and leverage.

—John Hagel III and Arthur G. Armstrong,
Net.Gain *(1997)*

If the 1980s were about quality and the 1990s were about reengineering, then the 2000s will be about velocity. About how quickly the nature of business itself will be transacted. About how information access will alter the lifestyle of consumers and their expectations of business. Quality improvements and business process improvements will occur far faster. When the increase in velocity of business is great enough, the very nature of business changes.

—Bill Gates, Business @ the Speed of Thought *(1999)*

Software is the competitive weapon of the new millennium.

> —*Ann Winblad, cofounder of the venture capital*
> *firm Hummo Winblad Venture Partners,*
> *in* The New York Times *(1997)*

If Microsoft made cars ... we'd all have to switch to Microsoft Gas.

> —*Po Bronson,* The First $20 Million Is Always the Hardest *(1997)*

According to the Meta Group, a research firm, nearly 90 percent of large organizations have some type of intranet.... It is difficult to precisely calculate the financial benefits of the impact of intranets. But companies that are investing heavily in them say their intranets are becoming essential for improving productivity, for reducing the costs of tasks like ordering business cards or publishing staff phone directories and for giving employees more autonomy and flexibility in how they do their work.

> —*Susan Stellin, "Intranets Nurture Companies*
> *from the Inside" in* The New York Times *(2001)*

If you have content, you need a network, and if you have a network, you need content.

> —*Thomas Niehaus of the consulting firm*
> *Simba Information, Inc., in* Fortune *(1995)*

The Internet is like Darwinism on steroids. You evolve or get eliminated.

> —*Raul Fernandez of the Web site design firm*
> *Proxicom, in* The Wall Street Journal *(1997)*

The Internet will be the business infrastructure of the twenty-first century. To subject it to as many as 30,000 taxing jurisdictions applying different rules of taxation would be a mistake.

> —*U.S. senator Ron Wyden, sponsor of the Internet Tax Freedom Act, in* The New York Times *(1997)*

Orwell's vaunted theory of language—including the idea that an elite would control thought by promulgating a jargon with fewer words and concepts—well, history sure has put the Kibosh on that one. Today the English language has more words than ever, including bazillions of computer terms that only nerds can understand, like *cool, uncool, way cool,* and, of course, *kewl.*

> —*Moe Myerson, technology company manager, in* Inc. Technology *(1996)*

Anybody who runs a successful high-technology company has to be an eternal optimist, has to be able to take his risks. You're constantly betting the future of the company. If you stop, if you lose your courage, you fail. No fax manufacturer in the world makes money.

> —*John Scully, then outgoing CEO of Apple, in* Fortune *(1993)*

The main reason so many people have lost jobs, been forced to change jobs, or been unable to upgrade their jobs in the last tumultuous decade is not a lowering of U.S. trade barriers. It's technology. A Mexican working at 75 cents an hour didn't take the job of our office receptionist; a microchip did— the one that separates the voice mail device in all our office phones. A Chinese making 75 cents an hour didn't take that auto worker's job; a robot did. A Brazilian making 75 cents an hour didn't take your neighbor's grocery job; a supermarket scanner did.

—Thomas L. Friedman, in The New York Times *(1997)*

The links between advertising and marketing and retail transactions are going to disappear. The Internet is going to become a channel of distribution.

—Russell Collins, president of the Fattal & Collins unit of Grey Advertsing, Inc., in Business Week *(1996)*

Whenever you have a hidden problem with a medium, you should have clever ways to turn that problem into an opportunity. That's what Michael Dorch advocates. He is publishing a high-quality electronic column and is building up a readership base the old-fashioned way—by finding and retaining interested readers. He writes about the topics he likes to consult in so that the contacts his newsletter creates may someday turn into a paying business for him. And you can build meaningful customer contacts through a Web newsletter, too—it's a surefire formula for attracting repeat visitors and building those fabled electronic relationships that everybody wants but so rarely achieves.

—Alexander Hiam, Marketing for Dummies *(1997)*

A traditional junk mailing is successful if it gets a response rate of 2 percent or 3 percent. On the Internet, you'll get a 100 percent response. And 90 percent of it will be, "Don't you ever do this to me again."

—Erik Fair of Apple Computer, in Fortune *(1994)*

With few exceptions, technology is not likely to be the most important factor in determining the commercial success of a virtual community. It is, in fact, a relatively small part of the total investment and operating cost. Early experiences on the network suggest that the key technologies required to address the four broad interaction needs of fantasy, interest, relationship and transaction are already in place. Technology innovation is rapidly addressing unresolved issues such as security and the need for metering software that measures who did what where on the network, a prerequisite for developing the member profiles that advertisers and vendors will use to target potential audiences and customers more precisely.

—John Hagel III and Arthur G. Armstrong, Net.Gain *(1997)*

In our experience there are three essentials—building culture, practicing a particular brand of leadership, and using a handful of management disciplines—to ignite the fire that is necessary to generate the loyalty and commitment, the energy and the courage, that are necessary to integrate the Internet and to continue to build a great company.

—David S. Pottruck and Terry Pearce,
Clicks and Mortar: Passion Driven Growth
in an Internet Driven World *(2000)*

When thinking and collaboration are significantly assisted by computer technology, you have a digital nervous system. It consists of the advanced digital process that knowledge workers use to make better decisions.

—Bill Gates, Business @ the Speed of Thought *(1999)*

I'm more interested in beating Microsoft than I am in beating Bill Gates.

*—Larry Ellison, CEO of the computer firm Oracle,
in* Time *magazine (1997)*

Another old rule that changed was the rule that the financiers who backed the company, and perhaps the CEO who steered it to success, made the most money and accumulated the most power. Anyone who bothered to read Netscape's prospectus discovered a curious fact. The venture capitalists on Sand Hill Road and the CEO, Jim Barksdale, owned a few million shares each . . . but the young engineers whom Clark had pulled together also became rich.

Clark also made certain that by far the biggest stake in the company—nearly one-quarter of the whole—belonged to Jim Clark personally. Clark became the valley's newest billionaire.

—Michael Lewis, The New New Thing *(2000)*

Laptops, cellular phones, wireless modems and fax machines may change the work environment for many professions, but they don't alter the thought processes that ultimately lead to breakthroughs. What these tools have done, however, is help extend the working day; in effect they have created a portable assembly line for the 1990s that "allows" white-collar workers to remain online in planes, trains, cars, and at home. So much for the liberating technologies of the information age.

*—"Technology and the Twenty-four-Hour Day"
in* The Harvard Business Review *(1996)*

In short, information and the mechanisms for delivering it underlie much of what defines business boundaries, stabilizes corporate and industry structures, shapes the organization, and drives competitive advantage. The concepts of value chain and supply chain focus our attention—quite usefully—on the physical sequence that defines a business or an industry. But it is information, flowing in the interstices of these chains, that really links them together and generates most of their competitive advantage and profit potential. Like the air we breathe, the importance of information is sometimes overlooked because it is so pervasive, so manifold and so obvious.

—Philip Evans and Thomas S. Wurster, Blown to Bits *(2000)*

There are a lot of people running companies in Silicon Valley who haven't had the experience of managing through both up and down markets.

—Sandra Kurtzig, founder and CEO of the software firm ASK, in In the Company of Giants *by Rama Dev Jager and Rafael Orti (1997)*

THE LAW, ETHICS, AND SOCIAL RESPONSIBILITY

But no management ever has the license to steal. Shareholders as owners have judicial recourse; they can sue for damages if they believe that management has violated the contract with owners. Such lawsuits frequently do take place, indicating that at least some owners are actually monitoring performance of management. Perhaps a more important check is the presence of competing groups anxious to take over the managerial function.

—*Jack Hirshleifer and David Hirshleifer,*
Price Theory and Applications *(1976)*

Honesty is for the most part less profitable than dishonesty.

—*Plato,* The Republic

In no discussion with corporate managers have I found any serious consideration that the same factors favoring their success may make it harder for others outside the corporate system to live their lives. The disappearing farmer and craftsman, the small businessman who can no longer make a living in competition with giant companies, do not figure in the thoughts of corporate managers. Few worry that the new technology they create does away with jobs, many low-level jobs. They may boast that they are creating new and better jobs in communications and data processing without considering that the displaced operators and counter check-ers may lack the education or aptitude for the new jobs. Instead, they think about the needy in terms of freeloaders, trying to get something for nothing.

—*Michael Maccoby,* The Gamesman *(1976)*

Glass, china and reputation are easily cracked and never well mended.

—*Benjamin Franklin (1706–1790)*

The investor stands at the juncture between the engine of the world's economy and the fuel, money. This is the reason that the way we invest today will shape the world we live in tomorrow. Investments are both the link and the engine upon which both commerce and finance rely. By not accept-ing responsibility for this, investors have built the world we inhabit. Today, the world is shrinking with so little time remaining. There are two basic reasons for integrating social or ethical criteria into the investment decision-making process: the desire to align investments with values and the desire to play a role in creating positive social change.

—*Amy Domini,* Socially Responsible Investing *(2001)*

Business success, whether for the individual or for the nation, is a good thing only so far as it is accompanied by and develops a high standard of conduct—honor, integrity, civic courage. . . . This government stands for manhood first and for business only as an adjunct of manhood.

—Theodore Roosevelt, in his fifth annual
message to the U.S. Congress (1911)

It ought to be fairly easy to choose between "right" and "wrong" in relying on moral principles. But big business activity often demands that we select from alternatives that are neither wholly "right" nor wholly "wrong."

—Preston Townley, CEO of the Conference Board, in The Wiley
Book of Business Quotations *by Henry Ehrlich (1998)*

Only the little people pay taxes.

—Leona Helmsley, former hotel owner

We want to catch the bastards [computer hackers] and show the rest of them that you don't screw with Citibank.

—Jim Bailey of Citibank, in The Wall Street Journal *(1995)*

Mr. Draper tutored Mr. Wozniak and Mr. Jobs in the art of programming their own blue notes, capable of gaining free—and illegal—access to the telephone network. The two novice entrepreneurs sold the blue notes door-to-door on the Berkeley campus, several years before they founded Apple Computer.

—John Markoff, "The Odyssey of a Hacker: From an
Outlaw to a Consultant" in The New York Times *(2001)*

Healthy businesses pay taxes. Healthy businesses create increased employment. Healthy businesses create an ambience that's much more attractive than the insecurities and tensions associated with weak businesses. So I believe it is my responsibility to bring together, and nurture, growing businesses that are healthy, and to get more businesses into that category while minimizing the businesses that are in trouble. . . .

Our largest shareholder by far is the U.S. government. They get billions in tax revenue from us and that's their dividend. They get more dividends than we pay out to all shareholders combined. I'm not criticizing that; I'm saying how positive that is.

—Jack Welch, CEO of General Electric,
in Jack Welch Speaks *by Janet Lowe (1998)*

The stereotypical hacker is the blue-mohawked kid on a skateboard. He is not your problem. These kids end up in the headlines because they get caught. The people stealing proprietary information are professionals, and they're much harder to catch.

—Richard Power, editorial director of San Francisco's
Security Institute, in The San Francisco Chronicle *(2001)*

In 1991, the Motion Picture Association of America rated only 16 percent of American movies as fit for kids under thirteen. Yet a PG film is more than three times as likely as an R-rated film to gross over a hundred million dollars at the domestic box office.

—Ken Auletta, "What Won't You Do?" in
The New Yorker *(1993)*

R.J. Reynolds Tobacco Co. believes firmly in its long-held position that "kids should not smoke." We stand behind our position by offering programs that supplement other youth nonsmoking efforts in schools, at retail [outlets] and in the home. These programs . . . reflect the many studies that show the key factors affecting youth smoking to be the influences of parents and family.

—*R. J. Reynolds company statement, in* Governing *(1995)*

To make sure your corporation starts on the right side of the law, heed the following guidelines:

- Call the secretary of state each year to check your corporate status.
- Put the annual meetings (shareholders' and directors') on tickler cards.
- Check all contacts to ensure the proper name is used in each. The signature line should read "John Doe, President, XYZ Corp.," never just John Doe.
- Never use your name followed by "d.b.a." on a contract. Renegotiate any old ones that you do.
- Before undertaking any activity out of the normal course of business—like purchasing major assets—write a corporate resolution permitting it. Keep all completed forms in the corporate book.
- Never use corporate checks for personal debts and vice versa.
- Get professional advice about continued retained earnings not needed for immediate operating expenses.
- Know in advance what franchise fees are due.

—*Rieva Lesonsky and the staff of* Entrepreneur
Magazine, Start Your Own Business *(2000)*

The insistent spur of American culture is the promise of success for all. . . . In a competitive system, you are seduced into cutting corners just as closely as your nearest competitor. The business philosophy of pragmatism—whatever works is good—has always endangered ethics by defining good in terms of the long-term profit-and-loss statement.

—*Richard M. Huber,*
The American Idea of Success *(1971)*

If I suspect someone of being less than totally forthright, I will have one or two of his expense reports sent to my office. Expense reports are like a truth serum.

—*Mark McCormack,* What They Don't Teach
You at Harvard Business School *(1984)*

American business did not cause what's happening in our inner cities and rural schools—the waste of so many young minds. World economic forces, technology, and demographic factors are at its root; but we all will be accessories if we do nothing to change things. None of us can escape the social costs and pressures this waste is generating.

—*Jack Welch, in* Jack Welch Speaks
by Janet Lowe (1998)

There is no such thing as a minor lapse of integrity.

—*Tom Peters, in* The Encyclopedia
of Leadership *(2001)*

Another way of describing the wretched of the earth is to define them as citizens of those countries that have been falling behind the economic levels of the West during the past four centuries. Between 1952 and 1972, the gross product of the advanced capitalist nations increased from $1.25 trillion to $3.07 trillion. The increment of $1.82 trillion was three and a half times the aggregate product of the underdeveloped world in 1972, which was $520 billion. Using constant (1973) dollars, the rich lands saw their per capita income move from $2,000 to $4,000. The major capitalist powers have two thirds of the globe's income, but only 20 percent of its population; the underdeveloped nations, with more than 50 percent of the people, have less than 13 percent of the income.

—Michael Harrington, A Vast Majority:
A Journey to the World's Poor *(1977)*

After a 1982 Japanese Air Lines crash, the company president visited the victims in the hospital and their family members, presenting a gift of cash. In 1987 JAL's president attended a memorial service for 520 people killed in a crash the year before, and all employees observed a period of silence and prayer. When things go wrong, it is usually up to the company president in Japan to assume responsibility, regardless of where the fault actually lies. This shows sincerity and the desire to make amends. Far from increasing liability, such corporate blame-taking actually reduces claims.

—Leonard Koren, 283 Useful Ideas from Japan *(1988)*

I believe it is a religious duty to get all the money you can, fairly and honestly, to keep all you can, and to give away all you can.

> —*John D. Rockefeller, founder of Standard Oil, in* In the Words of Great Business Leaders *by Julie M. Fenster (2000)*

But the real self—one's true nature—can't change color to suit its environment. In any ongoing business situation, sooner or later—either subliminally or out in the open—you are going to find that you are dealing with that real person's self.

Weak closers tend to get stuck on a position. Strong closers always seem to find a solution. The approach may not be the original one, but it gets to the desired result. Strong closers are generally people who accomplish tasks on time. Weak closers often are consummate procrastinators. Grand closers rejoice when a deal closes. Weak closers feel a sense of loss when the project comes to an end.

> —*Michael C. Donaldson and Mimi Donaldson,* Negotiating for Dummies *(1996)*